ORGANIZED CHAOS, TIMES & PLACES

A Journey Through Life in Poems and Prose

JAMES A. MOODY, SR.

Copyright © 2025 James A. Moody, Sr.
All cover art copyright © 2025 James A. Moody, Sr.
All Rights Reserved

No part of this book may be reproduced or transmitted in any form or by any means, electronic or mechanical, including photocopying, recording, or by any information storage and retrieval system, without permission in writing from the author.

Library of Congress Control Number: 2025916593

Publishing Coordinator – Sharon Kizziah-Holmes

Indie Pub Press
Springfield, Missouri

ISBN -13: 978-1-964559-85-8 Paperback
ISBN -13: 978-1-964559-86-5 Hardback
ISBN -13: 978-1-964559-87-2 eBook

Freedom is not worth having if it does not include the freedom to make mistakes.

Mahatma Gandhi

TABLE OF CONTENTS

Acknowledgments	i
Red Face	1
Lazarus and the Rich Man	8
Perfection	11
To Be Female	12
The Guitar	14
Morning	14
Seasons	15
First Snow	16
Hurry Spring	17
I Lost a Friend	18
Ebbing Strength	20
Come Help Us	21
Going Home	22
Freedom	23
Flasher	24
The Finale	25
Planning	25
Searching	26
Painted Pictures	28
The Empty Room	29
The Pie Not There	30
Rebirth of Love	32
Love	33
Forgiveness	34
The Single Path	35
Procrastinate	36
Cold and Lonely Nights	37
Playing Hooky	38
I Love You Daddy	40
Cup of Coffee	41
I am	42
Finding Me	46
To Be Free	48
Dropped Defenses	50
A Child's Fate	51
Where I've Been	52

Floating	54
Conclusions	55
Steps of Searching	56
Faith	57
Like Jesus?	58
Searching For God	60
Knowing Wrath	62
I Met a Man, I Met God	64
Cry for Help	67
Fragile Truth	68
Remembering	68
The Verdict	69
Time in Hell	70
Choices	70
Smoke	71
Trust	72
Hands	73
Family Tree	74
Resignation	75
Disgrace	76
Heaven's Vote	76
A Summer Day	77
Spring Storms	78
Selfish Caring	79
I Will Not Cry	80
Saying Goodbye	81
Tomorrow Is Now	81
Diamonds of Promise	82
Guilty Rage	82
Missed Opportunities	83
Closing Down Life	83
The Search	84
The Testament	84
Winter's Hell	85
The Treasure Chest	86
End of the Line	87
All the Same	88
Clear to See	89
Still Here	89

Growing in Bible Wisdom	90
Home	91
The Victim	91
Worn Paths	92
Here in Hell	93
Unanswered Questions	94
Missing You	95
Communication	95
Heaven's Shame	96
Discovering God	96
Untold Secrets	97
Who Am I	98
The Reaper's Talent	99
If I Had Only Known	100
Dare to Question	101
Rewards	102
Learning Grace	103
Waiting Room	104
Lessons in Hope	105
Selling a Soul	106
What is in a Color?	107
Filling a Void	108
Fading Visions	109
Sign Post	110
Aloof	111
Enigma	112
Dancing Stars	113
Quick to Judge	114
Mom	115
Phobia	116
Fading Life	117
Becoming a Man	118
Public Opinion	119
Saying Goodbye	119
The Pinnacle of Knowledge	120
I Cannot Let it Go	123
Child in Need	124
Rewards Of Life	124
The Folly of Youth	125

The Eighth Deadly Sin	126
Buried Treasures	126
Cancer	127
Denial	127
The Bliss of Stagnation	128
Escaping	129
Escaping Self	130
A House of Words	132
Assessing Values	133
Real Men Cry	134
To Be a Man	136
The Cycle of Seasons	137
Would You Stop For Me	138

Acknowledgments

I would like to thank all the people who have come into my life and have inspired me to tell the stories in poetic form.

Thank you, Venessa, for the editing work you have done to help me get this accomplished.

Thank you, Sharon, for the publishing work.

I especially thank Kristi for the encouragement, along with giving useful input and beneficial suggestions, in both writing and publishing.

RED FACE

"Welcome," reads the invitation stenciled on the floor,
"Come in and pass some time with us," is written on the door.
"You might enter as a stranger, but you will leave us as a friend,
This promise is our guarantee
That you'll come back again."

The young man steps inside the bar to a soft and pleasant pulse,
To conversations of current events and marketing results.
Sliding into an empty booth, he asks the waiter for a brew,
Friendly nods from those around
Affirms the "Welcome" sign is true.

Gathered friends in the corner booth bade him not to sit alone,
"Come join the celebration," they cry in a celebrating tone.
An exchange of names and temperaments, friendships quickly form,
The atmosphere is light and lively
The mood is generous and warm.

The young men share histories as each buy rounds of beer,
More than just the day's events they speak of deepening fear.
Of a world that has gone amiss and is headed for a fall,
They talk of how the game is rigged
And their backs are against the wall.

A fifth drink is all but gone as his sixth is set in line,
The young man, in deep discussion, has lost his sense of time.
The hour is late and many beers the patrons have consumed,
The atmosphere, though still quite calm
Holds a sense of pending doom.

Those conversing with the youth, express intent to leave,
Masculine courtesies are exchanged as garments are retrieved.
The subject of a worsening system they all agreed as true,
Was shared only with those now leaving
But the young man isn't through.

Now that the newfound friends have each gone their way,
The young man resolves within himself he is yet to stay.
Numbly comfortable, well relaxed, not ready to go home,
Another beer of gathered confidence
He's left to sit alone.

Above the rising drunken utterances one voice is clearly heard,
An older man of red complexion seems to be perturbed.
His rising rant, he lost some money at the closing of the day,
Of the markets he'd invested in
One had gone astray.

Bolstered bravado prompts the youth to express his point of view,
"Friend be of cheer, do not fret for tomorrow is always new.
Markets rally and prices rise, you'll gain what you have lost,
And even should that fail to be
Is your fretting worth this cost?"

The old man scans a squinted search, to learn who speaks to him,
His vision settles on the youth; he responds with gnarled grin.
"Who are you to advise on life, you're just a sniveling pup,
Did your parents not teach you well
That it's rude to interrupt?"

"I've been around a lot of years and have lived a varied life,
It's by my wit that I've survived and prevailed in every strife.
Again, I ask why you presume to advise me on anything,
You're but a fledgling who's not yet ready
To depart your mother's wing."

"The markets I've invested in have all been paying well,
Adding to my collective wealth at every closing bell.
Acquiring gold is the ambition of we who play the game,
Where getting more is our intent
Someday you'll feel the same."

"What is fair," the youth injects, "is we share in what is ours,
Not this system that rewards only those of wealthy powers.
Our planet is our only vessel on which we each rely,
No single one has greater rights
On who should live or die."

"If our world were just you and I afloat in endless seas,
Better that we share our bread, than only one appeased.
What is fair for you, is right for me, and this should never fail,
I know that which would grieve my heart
Should pain your heart as well."

"It's man who made the rules that defends the greed of one percent,
Legal by the code *they* made of which *they* never will repent.
Yet just because it is a law it does not mean *their* law is right,
To starve the weak and helpless many
And justify their plight."

The older man is not impressed with the reason of the youth,
He considered what the boy had said then offered this excuse.
For why the kid failed to see the truth so well defined,
But now the old man thought his duty
To correct the young man's mind.

"I know what's right, I'll tell you so", declares the red-faced man,
"It's not my fault you're dull of sense and have yet to understand!
The facts are there for all to see yet you my witless friend,
Seem deluded in your hopes and dreams
In a world of *let's pretend*."

"My friends and I do not relish your judgement of our means,
The system to which we adhere is fair, concise, and clean.
We've traveled roads in our time you have yet to see,
When you denounce what's long established
You're denouncing more than me."

"There was a time I was like you where ignorance was my fate,
An anxious view of what was wrong and ready for debate.
It was my dream to fix a system, slanted and unjust,
As luck would have it my errors were caught
It's now the system that I trust."

Confident in his proclamations, his defense of hallowed truth,
Red Face bows in mocked aplomb yielding to the youth.
"What challenge now will you espouse refuting me who's wise,
I declare your words defeated
Your truths are now your lies."

With knitted brow the young man considers the words of old Red Face,
Hoping not to fan the anger he replies with gentle grace.
"I respect you sir, you're thrice my age, maybe even more,
I will not dispute your words, my friend
Your forgiveness I implore."

"Was not my aim to rile you sir, I thought to ease your stress,
Because your time of learning's more, it's you who must know best.
I concede my friend to your many years of life,
It is I that could gain from you
In seeking your advice."

"That is, of course, if my pursuit were to play the slanted game,
Where all is never quite enough for those who have no shame.
The golden rule is a code that should measure every deed,
How could I live in such opulence
When so many are in need?"

Red Face is rankled at the subtle response so curt,
Before his peers the young man mocked him, his ego has been hurt.
With fists clenched and rigid jaw, he holds his mounting rage,
Rising slowly from his stool
Again, taking center stage.

His back turned toward the youth to punctuate his contempt,
Old Red Face swears not to stop till all his ire is spent.
"You ignorant insolent bastard, you are so quick to quip,"
Spitting out his venomous words
"You're a spineless little shit!"

Turning slowly, his eyes ablaze, as red as is his face,
He scans the bar and all his friends of this favored drinking place.
"I knew you lacked the grit my boy, so easy to defeat,
Now apologize to these my friends
Or we'll take this to the street."

Silence falls upon the room as all strain to hear the youth,
To his feet the young man rises stepping from his booth.
"I will not engage in violence on this you can depend,
And neither will you touch me, Sir
For with words, I can defend."

"It matters not what we opine for truth is carved in stone,
Opinions are all we have; we each have but our own.
Mentors who did quell your dreams, so as never to be heard,
Stifled youthful aspirations
Pronounced them as absurd."

"I pity that to you this happened for you're loyal to their creed,
An ideology of free market awash in utter greed.
Now you're aged, your ways are set, and can't bend with the wind,
I'm sorry, Sir, you will not see
And believe that I *pretend*."

"It is not your worth, the man you are that I have put in question,
You have your story, as you've lived, on these I make no suggestion.
The deeds you've done whether kind or rude to those in your extent,
    Speaks the value of your soul
    And how your life is spent."

The truthful words the young man spoke Red Face will not hear,
Unbridled fury consumes his heart to him his course is clear.
"Who are you, you son-of-a-bitch to tell me I lack sense,
    What I believe I know is truth
    It's you who will repent!"

"I'll kick your ass, I'll beat you down, a fate you've earned from me,
Not one of these my friends around will aid your plight, you'll see!"
Red Face lunges toward the youth but the young man steps aside,
    Crashing to the barroom floor
    Red Face clutched his chest then died.

The ashen youth agape and staring, Red Face prostrate on the floor,
Oblivious to the barroom murmurs now rising to a roar.
Indignation their time of leisure disrupted by this event,
    The one to blame is this young man
    And their anger will be spent.

Dragging him into the street as Red Face had threatened to do,
The crowd does vent their shock and rage, when it is finally through.
The young man lay with bloodied face and cannot be recognized,
    The crowd steps back silently watching
    As the young man dies.

A darkened silence settles over as the young man breathes his last,
A realization of what they've done now that the moments passed.
One guilty of this evil act voiced the thoughts of all the rest,
    "We now must lie to save ourselves
    Or everyone confess."

No one dared to look at the other as they each go their own,
No words are spoken, no pairs of friends, each walk away alone.
Someone summons those in charge to come investigate,
The barkeep stands behind the bar
The only one who waits.

The inquest of the night's events was simple, short in time,
Some of those who did the deed were witnesses to the crime.
A man was slaughtered, robbed of life, yet no one bears the blame,
The only punishment to those who care
Is each their sense of shame.

What could have been so important to cost the lives of two,
And bring about the crime of murder, on those that Red Face knew?
Nothing more than politics of what is right and fair,
The young man braved to question
Equal rights in all that is shared.

Lazarus and the Rich Man

I am Lazarus who sits and waits,
By this ancient crumbling gate.

Watching each one as they pass by,
I often times intone my cry.

For alms of pity on my woeful frame,
My rags of filth compound my shame.

Of those who care to know my name,
Except for them, all else the same.

Still, I sit outside this gate,
Beg for mercy then wait and wait.

Comfort found in words that tell,
Denouncing life in fiendish hell.

Search deeper in the err of lore's,
Confront the lies that shield deplores.

That life is blessed, a gift to take,
Yet mine too grievous to contemplate.

For as the shadow of time lays straight,
What truth there is beyond this gate.

Where theories and assumptions crumble,
For those who dared to not be humble.

Desolation of their ivory towers,
The lies of truth are soon devoured.

Naked, shed of all their glory,
Now will tell another story.

The rich exalted kings of earth,
Are given yet another birth.

Devoid of all their airy heights,
Where having gold assures all rights.

Begin to know the pains of squalor,
Their lofty towers they watch grow smaller.

More than just beyond their reach,
Their cries for mercy do impeach.

The lives they lived lacking shame,
For never having known my name.

It is I that now sit atop the tower,
Watching those who hide and cower.

Life with barbs that sting the soul,
With nothing left to help console.

Having been where they are now,
Doesn't give me joy somehow.

Lamenting the pain they feel,
For I too well know it's real.

What makes the difference in them and I,
Is nothing more than knowing why.

The mournful cries they emit,
Yet never having spoke of it.

I know intimately of life so hollow,
Never sure which path to follow.

From paradise with Abraham,
I want to help them see the plan.

They are me and I am them,
From here is where we start again.

The right of all to stand together,
Complete equality of one another.

A brotherhood/sisterhood that will expand,
Across the shores of time and land,
Because at last we understand.

PERFECTION

A rose of precise symmetry
Bears petals crimson deep
In gardens of true unity
Rewards of labor's reaped

A birth of pure and simple grace
Born out of love for beauty
Fills a void as common place
Assigned the joy of duty

Emerging from the dark of night
Bejeweled with drops of dew
Framed in morning's golden light
Reflects of rainbow's hue

On canvas of a cloudless sky
Ascends from misty haze
An image from on heaven's high
Exquisite on which to gaze

Fragile is this pristine view
A scene of spotless token
Oh, that when the seasons through
It not lie sad and broken

Delicate in its fine details
With no thoughts of protection
An evil wind embarks, assails
Destroyed that was perfection

TO BE FEMALE

Indentured chattel, owned to service
To bear the master's seed
Self-expression long traversed
Catering to master's greed

Efficaciousness wanes to diminished state
Turned out to an unknown chance
A fresh replacement stands in wait
Eager that they advance

Time moves on and change is known
Their property grows to self-aware
Defies the order to stand alone
As masters are forced to fair

The steady push to have a voice
Gains freedom to rise and stand
At last, the masters have no choice
Rescinds his ruled command

As goods no longer made to endure
Yet controlled in veiled disguise
Unscrupulous powers still assure
Subordinates must comply

Though laws applied are made a must
Compelled by proposition
Yield to that of such disgust
To secure a worth position

Of all those of each our lives
That should hold utmost esteemed
Mothers, daughters, sisters, wives
Must never be demeaned

Parity demands to give respect
Coequal but not superior
Master's rule has no effect
His place exposed inferior

THE GUITAR

Silent beauty rests alone confined devoid of purpose
Reflecting of the days that were, radiant in its form
Fingered wear, marks of strumming strokes
Though intact as was designed
Only half of what was to be
Only half of that gift to give
Alone it sits, alone it rests in the empty room
No metered strums or precise placed fingers performed in unison
It's quiet now, no serenade to fill the heart with glorious sound
The other half is quiet too as they lay beneath the ground

MORNING

A faint glow of light crests the distant horizon transforming the stillness of night into a chorus of warbling celebration as the day creatures trumpet the arrival of the fresh unmarked canvas upon which tomorrow's history will be inscribed. The cockerel's cry pierces the lingering ink of night, inviting the light of day to cast its long shadows towards the fading darkness. A lone tree silhouetting its leafless skeletal remains standing starkly against the orange of dawn half buried in the waning mist of daybreak.

    The frost-covered brittle grass snaps and crunches beneath the weight of approaching footsteps. Clouds of breath vanish into the frigid morning air as the day creatures stir to find their place.

SEASONS

Fading green of tiring leaves
Arid winds stir lofty trees
Beneath a dome of cloudless sky
Summer breathes and heaves a sigh

Northern winds push boughs to bend
Summer struggles but fails to win
Returning days of borrowed light
Leaves of crimsons and yellows bright

The demise of fall drifts to earth
Much that spring had given birth
Winter's snow blankets grief
Hides the death that lies beneath

Distant thunder, warming ground
Trumpets life to rise, rebound
Claims the brightness of the sun
New life cycles have begun

Thriving busy spins of new
Making life and then is through
Freshness wanes to ashen pale
Standing shadows reverse their trail

Fading green of tiring leaves
Arid winds stir lofty trees
Beneath a dome of cloudless sky
Summer breathes and heaves a sigh

FIRST SNOW

Rain began to fall in early evening, a blessing of showers long overdue and deeply appreciated. The tapping of the rain serenaded into an early sleep. Sometime after midnight the rain gave way to the muffled silence of falling snow. The day dawns upon a world of white contrasted by the shadows of darkness where the snow could not reach. The glow of pinkish orange reflecting off the cover of pure white as the sun waits to crest the horizon. The framed view from the upstairs window is reminiscent of long ago Christmas cards. Tree limbs supporting mounds of snow bowing under the weight. The north facing side of tree trunks are half encircled with the clinging snow. Winter has made her debut, two days late of the assigned calendar date but nonetheless she has arrived.

HURRY SPRING

Cool and crisp, the morning air
Springtime drawing near
Undecided, uncommitted, unrelenting
Battles over land dominion
Rebirth or dormant state
Lies beneath the crust of cold
Anxiously awaits

Measured times of calculate
Marks of times approximate
Seasons set to clocks
Dependence ever mocks
Stay or leave does fluctuate
In days of new or days of old
Anxiously awaits

I Lost a Friend

I lost a friend from life today, from anguish unresolved
He wrestled with his demons of scattered puzzle parts, an equation left unsolved
He looked for God from light to dark, from child to aged old man
Why he gave up to nescience is hard to understand

The days were never long enough to search out every clue
Lasting answers never came, his disappointments grew

Fading hopes wore him down in his struggle to find truth
He wanted to see the face of God, an ambition from his youth

The search had become the cause, a chance to know what's true
A path that extends an untold grace that always stands anew

An embrace to break the coldness of the fragile and frightened soul
To steal a touch of healing that could make his spirit whole

The questions never stopped coming as they filled the shortening days
Did he cry real tears as he touched the gun, determined not to stay

He couldn't take the answer 'no' though he heard it so much before
Quietly he stole into his room and silently locked the door

Did he think of who'd clean up the mess, the spattered blood and hair?
Did he feel in every way there was no one left to care?

Surely there is a special place in God's heart for those who can't go on
The face of life so bitter to rather just be done

Those who find life so void of hope sometimes choose to leave
And we that stay to help and hold anguished as we grieve

Dedicated to Mark

Ebbing Strength

The lamp burns strong, sufficient of fuel
Illuminating plights ahead
Replenished reserves of strengths to rule
Conquering feats of dread

The wick is measured, the only one
Conveys the source of strength
Is always spent when tasks are done
Shortening of its length

Is only discerned by passing of years
Compared from first to last
Then comes the time that it appears
Its worth is all the past

The light now flickers with pulsing flame
From stable to questioned strength
The conduit of talent and fame
Is waning too in length

A sputtering strobe of final brilliance
Extinguishing visual aid
No longer holds a power of resilience
As smoking spirits fade

COME HELP US

A mindful reach for spirit's care
Secrets kept that they might share
To know the answers hidden there
Yet not to search I could not dare

The freshness of a budding leaf
In time will end in winter's grief
A life that's spent and one so brief
Encouraged hope in trust's belief

Muteness holds its icy grips
No truths allowed of silence slips
Hopes and doubts do rise and dips
And still no sound escapes your lips

GOING HOME

I find that now this day is here
Adrift in search of land
A harbor from the final tempest
I need a place to stand
I bear no gift or talent
With which to pay my way
Accountability for myself and more
Are words of yesterday

It was never my intent
To weave this path alone
Searching through a clouded hope
Of more that's yet unknown
Words that soar above the din
Of precision and well defined
Floating to receptors
Standing ready by design

FREEDOM

Sentenced to a life of lone confinement
Our crime is that of simply being born
Fate dictates the wards of our assignment
A charge to which our jailers have been sworn

A first the walls that define our spacing
Consisted of the nurture that we persist
Though not yet perceived as so embracing
In time restrictions demand we not resist

Imprisoned as Papillon at Devils Island
With liberty to roam from shore to shore
But to sail in search of a new land
Bound to ocean's borders and no more

When we've served a life's sentence
The verdict of a new crime to condemn
Notwithstanding the depths of our repentance
A death sentence is our final end

One Sunday morning, a family friend stopped by to visit my mom. I sat in the living room half listening to the friend relate what had happened to her the previous night. She had been at the local laundromat doing the family wash when...

FLASHER

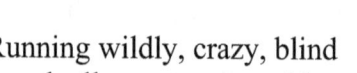

Running wildly, crazy, blind
Through alleys, streets, and lanes
The deed just done, the evil crime
An act of one insane

The moment past, yet lingers still
A throbbing pounding sound
A time's supply of lasting thrill
Still fears he could be found

Returning to that passion'd night
A fantasy well known
Old woman in a laundromat
At work and all alone

Silently he steals inside
Unseen, a shadow's cloak
Old woman tries the sight to hide
His gaping overcoat

THE FINALE

The time to sow has spent in days, now is the time to reap
Gathered moments at journey's end holding fast to keep
Forgotten acts of such defile covered by opposing veil
Broken promises and shattered dreams, times where love did fail

Memories of those sacred times that swell the heart in pride
Reminiscence of tender moments time attempts to hide
Promises of a lifelong union, an alliance of vested trust
Fills the vault of treasured hopes lies covered in the dust

PLANNING

I thought to rule this day with intended purpose so when evening came, I could reflect upon the accomplishments of reasoned strategies. But morning soon filled with distracting cares that robbed the clock of time and then the morn was gone. Afternoon was projected as a clear field of uneventful freedom, an expanse of borderless opportunities sure to allow accomplishments of unmatched achievements, thus garnering unto myself a coveted sense of sagacious success. Ah, but this too was not to be for the once clear horizons began to gather the clouds of despair as the cares of life spoiled across the intended intentions leaving in its wake the ruins of my purpose of the day.

SEARCHING

Escaping from the endless same
Exiting from the day
Abandoning all those faceless names
The chance to get away

Shadows creep as daylight fades
The streets become a terror
Doors are locked with lowered shades
There's nothing left to share

Time is now where charades are played
To chase away the fears
A costly price that's never paid
Echoes of empty cheers

Pleasures known of wrong or right
As the sounds of search goes on
Lonely creatures of the night
Scream out their soulful song

Then prevailing silence seeks its place
As day does seek her own
The sight of all the endless waste
Of searching is now known

But what of cause, why is it so
The crime, the search, the deed
What is this truth left yet to know
That answers each soul's need

Is there a way that makes it right
To search in light of day
For answers hidden by the night
Of why we live this way

We toil for gold and money
That fills the void of light
To finance the longing journey
Of searching through the night

While faces hollow with despair
Frame eyes of hidden pain
The justice in and of what is fair
That never knows the shame

Unopened doors from which we choose
A fate to each be known
Some of us will win, will lose
While reaping what we've sown

Painted Pictures

A poem is a picture painted in the mind
Suspended in the moment of thoughts of every kind
As prose or metered measures arranged so as to tell
Of objects, cares or worries, of heaven or of hell

In words, a journey travels to places far and near
And fills the hearts of travelers where discoveries appear
Or defines long passed moments chiseled fast in stone
In places of congested crowds or standing all alone

Or describe the fate of love defined as loss or gain
Memories one celebrate or thoughts of deep disdain
And at the poem's conclusion the visitor can know
If where the words have taken them was where they meant to go

THE EMPTY ROOM

A single chair no longer there
Nor pictures to adorn the walls
One lone window lights the way
Illumes the dust that falls

Pale shadows where portraits hung
Hint of past lives and joyous times
Only traces of those who were
That's now left all behind

Beyond dirty panes of glass
Cold winds stir naked branches
Projecting shadows upon the walls
That dips in swirls and dances

Reminiscing of lives gone by
So sad with extreme gloom
Step back and close this door forever
On a cold and empty room

THE PIE NOT THERE

Occasion had that I should visit
A friend who was detained
And even though the visit was pleasant
I departed with nerves so strained

You see my friend did overdose
On pills and alcohol
Staggered into a leaning post
And had a nasty fall

Because the mixture is ill advised
And people often die
The objections she verbalized
Were simply passed on by

Strapped tightly to the ambulance gurney
Rolled quickly to the street
A continued part of a lifelong journey
Of addictions to defeat

Lest I wander too far away
From where this poem's going
Back to the story of visit day
Where my anxiety was growing

As I was leaving the halls of nine
A ward for those insane
I thought all was going fine
Till this gray sweet lady came

As though cradled in her upturned hand
She offered me some pie
At first, I didn't understand
But the twinkle in her eye

Let me know she wasn't there
But at her family farm
I thanked her offer of pie to share
And touched her on the arm

"It looks so good," I showered praise
"I'm really tempted so,
But too much work fills my days
I really have to go"

She said "okay" she understood
And turned yet toward another
I heard her say, "Oh I wish you would"
Like any loving mother

A corner turned, my exit made
In my car I sat and wondered
Not knowing why my nerves were frayed
My thoughts were torn asunder

Then the reason so clear to see
Most know what is and isn't real
I cannot know except for me
What others see and feel

Dedicated to Mickey

REBIRTH OF LOVE

Fondness stirs the heart to quicken
Inclines the quest for passions
Summons dread for those been stricken
To barter for concessions

Return to spirits, acquired devotions
Assign a trust restored
Fend off the strife of bruised emotions
Resign to that's adored

Doubt demands consuming fears
A terror that won't be stilled
Robs affection as it appears
Of strength the heart has willed

Binary is the path of choice
Should preference have discretion
Confront with anguished warning voice
The hell of fear's oppression

Dare to engage that sacred berth
Defy the fortress of lore
Think not to enter in frivolous mirth
To concede to chance once more

LOVE

"I love you," verbalized words stated and repeated millions of times every day the world over by untold numbers of people. The sentiment is universal, spoken in every dialect.

Three simple words are often the vessel that carries volumes of sentiment based upon time and experience or shared associations through circumstances. Familiarity and trust have weathered the test of failures, reinforced and fortified in mutual victories, thus bonding acquaintances into lasting commitments.

"Love," a four lettered word that transcends and soars above the degradation and trials of daily life, often the only vestige that makes everything else tolerable.

Yet this simple word is often used to the degree that much of its value is reduced to an expressed recital of obligatory responses to echo the statement of another. The returned proclamation is not worthy of such sentiments unless it is truly expressing the contents of a heart that is in love.

"I love green fields decorated with wildflowers," is not the same as "I love you as the gift that so gladdens my soul and decorates my existence with joy and the promise of hope."

FORGIVENESS

How I wish you could have known me
The person that I've been
So perhaps you could have shown me
Your love I could not win

The days of years that build the past
We've lived so much apart
And now I know time won't last
Too late to know my heart

So, when I ask to try and mend
The rift charged to my name
I've not much time until the end
To deal with this deep pain

So, listen please and know it's I
That speaks to you my friend
Forgive my wrongs before I die
None of which I can defend

It's not for me, though just a bit
That I ask you grant me pardon
For in the grave no lamps are lit
A field of lifeless garden

I ask you to accept my repentance
For you have more days still yet
That we not part still in defiance
That might cause you regret

THE SINGLE PATH

The twists and turns to here and now
Were most without selections
So, waste no time in musings
Of 'what if' as reflections

Had not the path to turn left or right
Or the choice that's most alluring
Would not have arrived at this place
Confirmed though not assuring

So, when temptations do arise
To explore to change regret
Yet also know that to this credit
We may well have never met

PROCRASTINATE

I walk a line and waste much time
That's cumbersome to navigate
Not that signposts are lacking here
But because I procrastinate

I claim the gift that's meant to uplift
To knowing of one's fate
But at day's end I question why
For still I procrastinate

And now this era has ticked to years
No horizons lie in wait
I reflect on days of yesteryear
I can no longer procrastinate

COLD AND LONELY NIGHTS

Children crying in the night
To sounds of merriment
Mother appears to quiet their fears
A moment too quickly spent

The sounds are loud then muffled
As the bar door swings wide then shuts
The people there don't seem to care
Those drunkards and those sluts

The cold car seat will not protect
Through the one thin blanket shared
Little brother's please do grieve
The older if he dared

To search and tell the mother
Of the dark consuming fright
Yet like before, there's only more
Of the cold and endless night

Those nights that pass for the child
Are longer than the days
Of warm sunshine and happy times
The anguish of it stays

The child now grown to man
Is strong and knows no frights
Still deep inside he tries to hide
From cold and lonely nights

Playing Hooky

A coughed complaint, "I think I'm sick"
Though Mother knows that it's a trick
She listens as if heard anew
And when my pleading scheme is through
Her feigned words of reproved assent
Are never held to be as true
Cause in her heart she does relent
As I always know she'll do

Big Brother with his own approach
Appeals to gain without reproach
Consent the same as is for me
A warm spring day that's school free
Still, there's a lesson to be learned
Though not in class where we should be
But by exploring the day's concern
No one else but Bro and me

The old gray barn becomes our fort
A bastion of unmatched import
Where encompassed by an imposing foe
We bravely fight, myself and Bro
And when it seems that all is lost
Though neither willing we let go
Too dear we know will be the cost
Except we try we'll never know

Images of our conjured rivals
Those we battle for our survival
Quickly vanish like winter steam
"Hey Brother, did you hear something?"
Before an answer it comes again
No, it's not a daytime dream
Grandma says, "Its time, come in
And get your hands lunchtime clean."

We sat in silence, my Bro and me
Neither knowing what was to be
Sandwich finished and milk gone too
I didn't sense the day was through
Without a word we rose to leave
When Grandma caught me by the sleeve
"I think you boys should be ashamed
Missing school to play your games"
The scold from Grandma came at a cost
In that instant the mood was lost
Brother wandered off to his room
I followed him but not too soon
"You claimed sickness," Grandma said
"The place to heal is back in bed."

I Love You Daddy

I reach and take the hand, believing it belongs to you
In purest words of innocence, I proclaim, "I love you Daddy"
You don't respond and so I look up and much to my 8-year-old embarrassment
I discover the hand I've been holding is that of a stranger
I immediately let go and run ahead searching for the hand I had intended to hold

Many times, through the years
I'd reach and take that hand to lead
Rough and strong with work

Often times I watched, as you'd descend
Into a stupor with your friend
An amber colored liquid you'd defend
Then you'd stop just to start again

Childhood is filled with memories of reaching for that hand that often times was not there
I so wanted to be best friends
Yet not all the memories are bad, there were moments of fun and jocularity where you realized you had a wife and kids
Sundays of swimming at the river, evenings sharing stories at the dinner table, times where you and your siblings remembered adventures of your youth, tender moments when your mother, my grandma, was laid to rest
I watched you fail again and again, a story of a lifetime

That boy now hides within a man
Still sometimes reaching for that work rough hand
Though knowing helps to understand
Ever resigned to the fact he never can
And that boy who was of then
Will always wish what could have been.
Still ever trying to fill with joy
The longing heart of that little boy

CUP OF COFFEE

As the dark brown liquid drains
Exposing depth of cup
Appears a gathering of unknown grains
Of something to corrupt

Does that of what I see consist
Escaping coffee grounds
Or are those blacken bits a risk
Of bugs I've stirred around

I spit the brown revolting thought
Returning the unknown specks
In hopes that what was in the pot
Is not of deep regrets

I AM

Can I know how it is that you feel
Should I tell you what I see as real

Having been where you are now
Can mine become yours somehow

Does my journey to this time
Make yours any less than mine

Who can judge me from their faulty post
Am I not the one that knows me the most

Yet, for me to see me as I really am
I'd have to be a completely different man

I know I'm not gay
I know what I say

For what it is worth
That's it from my birth

I didn't choose; it was just me
Just who I happen to be

Did you choose
To lie or to lose

Did you hide your most
To make an untruthful boast

Did you decide you thought you should be
Heterosexual to be just like me

Cause if you didn't, you too must realize
If seeing yourself as though through my eyes

There's nothing of pureness for us to lay claim
If you and I are truly the same

Or did you
Before you were through

See a road filled with pain and much sorrow
Opt out for a less troubled tomorrow

After battling a grievous temptation
Much to your own consternation

Conclude to be homosexual
Was far too socially special

Decide just to hide
This thing you denied

And war against those others
To punish and make suffer

Did all these actions
Create such distractions

Veil the guilt of your shame
You ascribed to your name

But maybe one day
You'll throw it away

To family and friends come to the open
Still loved by them all is what you'd be hoping

The center most issue of this moral fight
Is to judge and to label who's wrong or who's right

Of what we all are and will ultimately be
Unclouded and clear, truths we'll all see

The choices you pride and think of as yours
To be as you want through perceptive powers

Never discerning from where you arrived
Those persons who cared that you have survived

Nurture and nature sums up who you are
As the scattering of fruit never goes far

Your story was written long before you came
The one thing undone was knowing your name

The color of hair, of eyes, and of skin
Was never your choice from beginning to end

No pictures were offered of parents to be
No way you can alter your ancestry

In keeping with what society sees
Did you choose of yourself what you would be

Was your sex orientation picked from a list
Or the choice of gender to be or resist

Was your stature and strength an item of choice
The shrill of your speech or the depth of your voice

If you are poor and low in your class
Or rich and successful, with no ceilings of glass

How did you arrive at your station in life
A wealthy free ride or through struggle and strife

Just be honest and then you might know
Of what you can claim as your choices and show

That all that you are was set from the start
And all that you've done is act out your part

Finding Me

Morning spreads its light of promise for seeing what is hidden
Shadows appear like object's spirits revealing their intent
The sounds of newness pull me back from the death of sleep
A day of hope or despair, the choice not ever mine

People I care about, still deep within themselves
I walk from room to room watching, remembering, hoping
To wake someone would be to pull them back to what is reality
I retreat and let them carry on in their world of dark escape

In the quiet of total solitude, I reflect on what and why
I measure things and turn them over searching for something missed
But most of all I look deep inside to try and see what truth is there
Too often I find nothing and wonder what others see to love

Yet sometimes deep within me there is another morning that
spreads its dawning light of promise
for seeing what is hidden
The darkest places then glow with truth and understanding
I know myself and love myself and hold me with tender care
For what too often is perceived as evil is simply a plea for acceptance

I am now one of those people I care about still deep within myself
And as I walk from room to room watching, remembering, hoping
Something wakes me and pulls me back to reality
Wishing they had retreated and allowed me to carry on in my
world of dark escape

Now back in quiet solitude I reflect on what and why
To measure things and turn them over, looking for something missed
To look inside and try and see who I have become
I see nothing and wonder what others see to love

To Be Free

Look at me and tell me
All you think you can
Do you see the frightened child
Or the aging man

What can you say of me
By looking in my face
Can you read each crease and fold
Or say my life has been a waste

Can you see the truth
Of who and what I've been
Do my eyes now faded dim
Show what my heart intends

Even if there's truth or not
That I was evil from the start
Can you know why I was me
And what was in my heart

Are my experiences also yours
To the degree you can say
Without the slightest hint of doubt
Why I am as I am today

If you can please let me know
Of your powers and the such
Cause I can't see what made me, me
And I want to very much

I beg of you to tell me why
I want those things I do
Forbidden answers on demand
Because I haven't got a clue

I didn't wake one morning
And decide on what to feel
From where I stood each breaking day
I *woke* to what was real

Explain to me, if you can
From where my anger came
How did I learn to hit and hurt
And those vicious verbal games

And when you've finished telling me
The reasons for who I am
Can you please append to this
A hope that I'm not damned

In my defense you need to know
My doors were marked 'unknown'
The portholes to my comprehension
Were clearly not my own

Truths I followed were never mine
But of those who claimed to know
To understand everything
And their seed was left to grow

I think you should also know
And I say this as your brother
Your path is yours and mine is mine
And we are not each other

For what we said and what we did
The deeds we hoped to hide
Will soon be drawn into the light
Where truth can't be denied

Yet when you see my wrongs so clear
Are much like those you've known
Our judgments held for one another
Are judging each our own

DROPPED DEFENSES

This morning, I ventured into that forbidden realm of emotional awareness. I often avoid going there because invariably I am rendered into the most embarrassing demeanor of shedding tears when revisiting forgotten memories of pain and disappointments. In turn, I attempt to lessen my display of sentiment with feeble efforts of jocularity often mocking my unflattering exhibition of unmanly sentimentality. I've frequently thought the quotation in the Scriptures should have read, "Jesus *embarrassingly* wept." Yet it is not for me to determine and even so, it is I who holds disdain for sharing heartfelt emotions that can result in such unflattering manifestations of childlike and feministic mannerisms.

A CHILD'S FATE

Is history fair in assigning grant
Names inscribed on slabs of stone
Notations of a life so scant
Or words of praise for those well known

Each and all debut as equal
Of noble birth or heritage shame
Is set to that of parentage sequel
In accordance to family's fame

Hidden in that face of innocence
The path to which a child will take
Determined road of what ascent
In which they're set in life to make

What unknown deeds lay in wait
Set to environments sure to form
Can be ascribed as destined fate
Or mimed response but never sworn

What channeled course defines direction
Those dictates of a subject's lot
Hate or grace of what proportion
Determines when and where or not

Reaching depths of deeds of scorn
With wicked archives of such defile
A child conceived to mothers born
Of innocence is yet beguiled

WHERE I'VE BEEN

I know what it's like to be of this age
Although I can't claim a status of sage
But I can reflect on the passing of time
Of this I can say and of this is all mine

Though foggy and dim are memories at three
Most like 'still' photos is all I can see
The life as a toddler yet I know of so well
By watching my grandkids is how I can tell

More recollections of four and of five
A budding new world to just be alive
Age six and seven memories are clear
New pressures of school and social peers

Remembrances of those sharp and defined
Some of these memories I wish were not mine
Turning eight and then nine is clearer even yet
Moments in detail, secrets long kept

When I turned ten was special and new
My digits of age had now become two
Eleven through twenty though jumbled and mixed
Those memories come back some firm and so fixed

Adventured new spheres awakened within
A whole different reason for looking again
What was rejected, now eagerly sought
Boundaries wide open where souls can be bought

I discovered that love can be hellishly cruel
To control or repress when used as a tool
Once the heart's broken though wounded still beats
What appears to be mended is never complete

I long often thought twenty-one I'll be free
Nothing between my freedom and me
I drank lots of beer, whiskey, and wine
I remember I thought 'this is a good time'

The foolishness of youth was soon left behind
I entered an age more serious of mind
Becoming a father is crystal and clear
I recall all the feelings, the joys, and the fears

To be forty and fifty and sixty I know
Watching my loved ones some wither some grow
Those older before me did feeble and die
The emptiness left can still make me cry

And that I am here this age I've become
I want you to know all you who are young
That where you are now is where I have been
And through my memories I can live it again

Though we each and all travel a road of our own
The milestones to pass with many unknown
Cause trust to be broken in what to believe
Young hearts that are open learn how to grieve

So, when you see me and revile at my age
A useless old man not one to engage
With nothing in common have we to share
But before I must go, if I may dare

Maybe, just maybe we might could be friends
At least for a while before it all ends
Cause I was once there where you still might be
And perhaps I could share what you cannot yet see

FLOATING

Adrift aimless in darkened sea
A painful truth to be set free
Uncharted course of endless days
No beacon's light to guide the ways
No land of hope is yet to be
As I drift alone in darkened sea

A flash of light, not certain though
A light from hope does sometimes glow
Sweeps along the far distant shore
To hope is not to hope for more
Oh, how I want to start to row
What I'll find not certain though

Young as I were or aged old man
Each year passed by in search of land
A shoreline glimmer of promised light
Then more appeared within my sight
Soon too many to understand
For the young of age or aged old man

It is said that hope can be found
All that's needed is to look around
I looked and looked with more than a glance
I even thought to give some a chance
But soon each one letting me down
Adrift still hoping, hope can be found

CONCLUSIONS

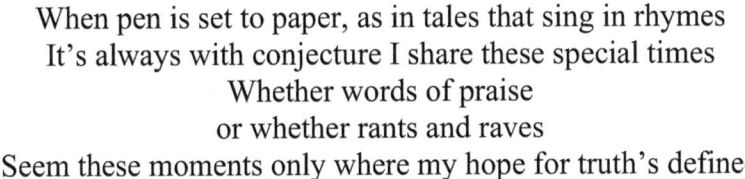

When pen is set to paper, as in tales that sing in rhymes
It's always with conjecture I share these special times
Whether words of praise
or whether rants and raves
Seem these moments only where my hope for truth's defined

Was left to me to search and see if through reason I could discern
Sift out those facts from what's assumed and hold to what I've learned
More than hope with no pretenses
and without distortion of defenses
Knowing truth matters most in ALL of life's concerns

My study time is near completion; it's time to test conclusions
Truths I've determined from this world of vast delusions
Whether scientist or religious sage
both claim to have the truth engaged
Yet neither can defend their concepts without mystic elusions

Would rather stand alas redeemed to life beyond tomorrows
For all the wages that's paid in pain a pitted path of harrows
To learn that all that's said and done
was empty hope for everyone
Then reasons here have cost too dear for all the loss in sorrows

Yet I must say that trust today is not lost in hopeless theories
Is my quest to put at rest through answers to my inquires
Still, there's truth that can be found
that often turns my mind around
Dispels the fears of what's unknown and strengthens a heart that's weary

STEPS OF SEARCHING

Morning invites adventure at the graying skies of dawn
Awakens within a spirit to explore another day
Pursuing secrets yet to know
That lay hidden deep within the undiscovered
A repeated journey retracing footsteps
From new perspectives of learned values
Hoping, believing truth lay beneath an unturned stone
Discovery that explodes into new perceptions
Unearthing the mysteries of God

I've passed this way, a trail of non-description
Trees and stones that stay in time
Familiar patterns of the forgotten
Differences recognized without form
An added layer of fallen leaves
A single sound, a place now silent
A mound of deer scat lining the trail
Time not yet known
All the same but moved beyond days gone by

Another dawning beckons the call of searching
I step into a world of pleasing mist
Enveloped into the gray shroud
Disappearance measured in footsteps
Swallowed in the confinement of limited visions
Remembering in frames with bordered walls
A coffee cup intended to be retrieved hanging on a tree limb
Left to a future that never happened
The deafening silence screams inside my thoughts
I walk alone

FAITH

I hope to not provoke Your ire
To inquire of our fate
Questions of which You must tire
To pass through heaven's gate

Or not to once incur Your wrath
By one so dull of sense
As I traverse this hidden path
Defining where and whence

Yet still I hold that need to know
Unsure what lies ahead
How to relent, to let go
An exit to my dread

In darkness still, next step I take
As a blind one peer
What evils I should dare to wake
Faithless in my fear

Alas You answer a vague unknown
A trust mantle to be worn
In faith is how the path is shone
Free of heaven's scorn

Again, I ask as if anew
Refresh my faith and trust
Till that day declares me through
Your guidance is a must

Like Jesus?

If I would be like Jesus
As is taught the way to be
Would I look upon the homeless
As something not involving me

Should I look with studied gaze
At this representative of *fail*
Know his life through his eyes
Discern what that life entails

Perhaps devoid of love from birth
A candidate for dazed distractions
Fleeing ties of disappointments
Searching out the wrong attractions

Deciding this, his life, his choice
Disavowing the poor man's plight
Can I now walk away guilt free
In believing that I'm right

Or just because the person
Who stands in front of me
Is not the class of person
I think he ought to be

He'd use the cash I'd give him
To buy himself a drug
Giving me the freedom
To leave him with a shrug

Or maybe I should consider
I can't know where he's been
The depths to which he may have sank
To judge him of his sin

Would I think myself so guiltless
As to stand for God to judge
Declaring, "I'm not like that man!"
For whom I hold this righteous grudge

If I should take another look
At the person standing there
Can I persist to demean his worth
Pronounce my judgment fair

To stop, to look, to see a man
A man who's much like me
Confined within his space of walls
And set adrift in open sea

Jesus said, what's done to Him
Is done unto the least
And so this man in front of me
Might be that man of peace

SEARCHING FOR GOD

———◆‹‹◆››◆———

I thought I'd look for God today
In places searched before
Hoping that I've missed a clue
Or find an unopened door

My search began with the morning news
For something to bring cheer
To let me know that God is real
I found only strife and fear

I peered into my own desires
For meaning in my pursuit
I found a lot of dread and doubts
And a self in deep dispute

I then turned to the Bible
For hopes that hope is well
Only to find in cryptic words
My destiny in hell

I looked to friends and neighbors
For some good news in their eyes
Their down cast face of sorrow
Told me they too realize

That God is either gone or not
His presence is not here
Today's the same as yesterday
As it's been throughout the years

But all those well-meaning folks
Tell me "have a little faith
And God will come and carry you home
To that peaceful loving place"

They say "it's faith that saves us"
But I can't see how that can be
For faith was never crucified
Nor died to set us free

No, faith is just for coping
With this helpless life of sin
An instrument for getting by
While waiting for the end

Faith fortifies our journey
So that we finish and not roam
It leads us through the darkened valley
Till we *all* are brought back home

I didn't find God today
No matter where I looked
Perhaps it's just my inept ways
Or a truth that was mistook

And tomorrow I'll begin again
To see what I might see
And maybe someday the time will come
When God will search for me

KNOWING WRATH

Regrets:

Yesterday I faltered in my hopes that You are real
I swore at You with threats of death
My own, for sure, because You cannot be touched

I plead:

Give me something to know, to live for, to look forward to
What is, is never enough
Don't You know how it feels to be all alone in the universe

I express:

Rage of fear and hopelessness
The horror of never knowing
How can You be so silent, how can You not understand

I surrender:

I wish You could see the real me
Take my hand in Yours
Tell me what to do
Tell me how to feel
For I feel all is lost
Without hope

I seek forgiveness:

I'm quiet now, the panicked rant has passed
Weary to the core
My desperation spent in fits of rage

I forgive You:

I wonder, would I have been one of them
That called out for You to die
It sure seems I could have been
Until I saw You cry

I Met a Man, I Met God

I once knew of a man
By the color of his skin
He lived in a part of town
Impoverished and so grim

Was easy to define him
As I watched the evening news
People aimed to hurt and kill
Losers born to lose

One day arriving at my work
I discovered him by my side
I studied him with stealthy caution
Pondering what crimes he had to hide

A morning nod soon gave way
To lunch time and every break
And as I grew to know the man
I recognized the vile mistake

He wasn't that gangster, murderer
That the news portrayed him to be
He spoke often of his private life
His wife, his kids, his family

I once knew of a man
By the label I put on him
A label that was so unfair
It never should have been

Those first days turned into weeks
And months and now to years
My preconceived beliefs of him,
My anxiety and my fears

Have long gave way to knowing him
As my brother, trusted friend
The ugly label I once used
I'll never use again

What is interesting to note
Is that *knowing* is the key
Labels of a vengeful God
Is what most people see

But what if God is not so angry
And ready to chastise
What if He is grieved for us
For believing in the lies

What if we are mistaken
About what is happening here
What if how we now view God
Has been distorted, made unclear

What if Jesus as the Son of God
Lived among us to understand
The emptiness apart from God
To be the Son of man

What if Jesus gave His life
Not as a ransom that was due
But to show beyond all doubts
His boundless love is true

What if God is victim too
As surely we must be
Of lies and broad deceptions
Where few of us can see

The Innocence of our Creator
And how He is without defense
To the challenge of His right to rule
Until every soul's convinced

Jesus is our Champion of truth
That was His mission here
To let us know the one true God
And we have no cause to fear

Condemnation was not His charge
Intended for us on earth
Rescue has always been
His expression of our worth

Knowledge is the key to truth
That makes us understand
Color has no place in judging
The value of any man

Fear of God is not the way
To mend the broke esteem
But loving Him as our Father
Is how we are redeemed

CRY FOR HELP

I need God to understand me better than I understand myself. I'm not looking to excuse my behaviors, I need Him to let me know what made me as I am. Obstinate to compassion, blinded to fairness, and unable to know how to love.

I need a father who can see
That the child I was, is still in me
For fear and sorrow, I did conceal
I had to hide the things I'd feel
I scream inside, unanswered plea
I watched as changes came over me
God told us all that heaven's gate
Is not for us to contemplate
Until we become as we had been
Before the scars of bearing sin
Again, the soul of we so young
Is what You say we must become
How can I change what life has made
Learn how to drop this forced charade
Unknow the things I've seen and done
Forgive myself for being one
Who could not bend to feign of trust
Not understanding why I must
Yet, if I can be stripped of shields
So the child I was can be revealed
Who cried when hurt from being sad
Then learned to hide by being mad
And how to mask and play the game
To never give up as if ashamed
Always hold emotions tight
Don't let them know my fear to fight

Fragile Truth

I muse upon reality to confirm the facts as fact
To find in singularity the tracks on which to track
I touch the dome of truth to break the tensioned sphere
And watch in total disillusion as it flows to disappear

Though the path of destination is weary and confused
It's worn to depths of travel and shows of being used
I trace the exit pathways of the sphere that has been spent
Believing the objectives are those of some intent

Yet upon a renewed adventure I recognize a course
What was once considered truth was resigned without remorse
The follies of the impertinent are futile and ornate
Fleeing from what's known as truth that's hard to undertake

Remembering

A walk of silent solitude through memories of what was. Some bring joy in hopes to come, yet sting the heart with barbs of truth that may well never be again. Recalling those times where the people who were a part of the moment, alive and vibrant, now expose the emptiness. A sigh of profound sadness extinguishes the remaining flames of hope. Only the thoughts of solace are held in the promise all good things will someday be restored to the sameness of those times.

The Verdict

Blind and deaf, confused and scared
I stumble through each day
Every step a challenge dared
Not knowing if I've strayed
A crooked winding twisted path
Forever fearful of incurring wrath

An image of a God to fear
Demanding and so stern
Defined in riddles blurred, unclear
A gift of life or something earned
A celebration of joyous news
Left in ruins and still confused

Abandoned lessons ingrained so deep
Forsaking what was known
Fearful of what was sown to reap
To stand in place alone
I hold my breath, I wait in dread
At last to hear my verdict read

TIME IN HELL

Rise above these depths of hell
No act of gaiety does dispel
Standing watch as life meets fate
Those who care do congregate
Counting breaths as they wait
At last will ring that final bell
Declares an end to time in hell

CHOICES

At most, as I can best recall, no quests did I submit
Nor offers as to what to choose or options to omit
A slow dawning to questioned facts was all that was to be
For most of what I understand confined to what I see

Had I not been introduced to hope designed of those before
I would have fashioned for myself answers through self explore
Of where and why from which we came or where we are to end
Determine truth based on knowledge on which I can depend

SMOKE

Trust and obey was the command of the day
To keep yourself pure was the only way sure
Never to drink or to smoke was a spiritual joke
A challenge to dare formed out of no care
Just a rule to defend to fashion your end
Avoid the assault that is of your fault

I didn't listen for something was missing
I did of my own and did it alone
I picked the route, and I was devout
I smoked and I drank were the depths that I sank
The road I walked was adverse to that taught
And now that I'm old my story is told

I'll suffer and die while knowing just why
I took the dread stuck in my head
The challenge was made to live up to their grade
Was diluted of fate I now know of too late
The reason to yield and just stay afield
Was to avoid in my death being starved for a breath

So now I can know of a demise that is slow
Each day that begins and stays till the end
A struggle to breathe that's never relieved
So, if told to obey as the only way
Think of instead a time that you'll dread
Just never do smoke for this death is no joke

TRUST

The rule of life does circumvent
Powers said to be
Strength and cause to repent
Unchained, unfettered, free

Was on a dreary day in time
Crossroads forced trust
One radiant of a glory shined
The others of a must

Reason battled o'er which to take
First the left, or then the right
Or neither, just to go on straight
I pondered long into the night

The cold of doubt closing in
I take a step, then back again
Being wrong my greatest fear
So, I remain stranded here

HANDS

Like most persons of my age, I have had multiple opportunities to view the still cold remains of a deceased friend or relative. The undertaker can usually make the cadaver look almost alive and sometimes healthy, but of course notwithstanding how good a job they can do is the knowledge the body in front of me is quiet, still, and no life is found within, cannot be ignored.

On numerous occasions, as I have scanned the still form of a deceased loved one, my attention would settle on the folded hands positioned comfortably across the abdomen. I would find myself anguishing over what a tragic loss in the perfectly formed and seemingly still fully functional hands now lying useless and never to engage in activity again. I would think what an awful waste of the creative tools soon to be placed into the ground and disintegrate into the dust of the earth.

I would especially anguish over the loss if I had a working knowledge of what those hands had been used for in life. Did the hands work in construction or were those hands adept at playing beautiful music through the instrument of their choice? Did those hands express loving tenderness with caressing strokes that transmitted the gentleness of the heart that guided them? Were they instrumental in healing or providing healthy benefits to those persons in their life? Did those hands love me, caress my soul with the care of love or did those hands reach out to help the lesser creatures?

I think of hands scarred with sacrifice for the benefit of humanity.

I know they are just hands and hands are of no use unless there is the person behind them guiding the actions. Yet, I grieve over the loss of the tools that expressed so much in life. I miss the hands of all those I love who no longer can express the contents of their heart.

FAMILY TREE

That fruit never drops far from the tree
Was not a statement I thought would fit me
But now I've aged and arrived at this place
It's a proven fact I now must face

You see up till now I refused to conform
To the patterning of truth, a cloak to be worn
Recognizing the traits of both father and mother
By watching the process in my sister and brother

"Not for me," I declared. My determined stout stance
I won't be like them, cause I'll give it no chance
But as of today, I glanced in the mirror
And what I saw there filled me with fear

The looks and attitude were so clear to see
That Mother and Father are a large part of me
Because this old knowledge has settled as truth
I now can celebrate what was rejected in youth

RESIGNATION

At morning's light I rise to meet the challenge of demand
A labor of an artist art to sculpt the dreams of man
Armored with the shield of purpose, intent on no refrain
The toils of yesterday lie in wait on which to build again

I garner all my strength, resolute to accomplish more
Add to all the tasks achieved, of all that's done before
I use the lessons learned from errors and of those misguided deeds
To know when and what to do to address advancement's needs

Then the day arrives where challenges cannot be met
And in the evening of that day, I retire in deep regret
Though adamant to rise above the failure of that darkened day
Again, and more, I fail the goal as my strengths are ebbed away

At last, the day of scorned detest proves me inept to rise
A fate I knew would one day be, a day of dread despise
For all the tasks accomplished and all that's gained to know
The accumulation of knowledge has long last ceased to grow

So, in the final analysis, those monuments I claim as mine
Were built upon the shifting earth and won't stand the test of time
All I've done, the knowledge gained, the wisdom of my years
Are laid in dust and die with me and washed away in tears

DISGRACE

I strived to build a pensive verse
Of Godly nature too
Contemplatively I searched my soul
Reaching for that reasoned place
The words were stuck in spectral hell
I relinquished in dark disgrace

HEAVEN'S VOTE

Was told that time was not my friend
To plan a future of long extend
Though today was mine to spend
There's no tomorrows to depend

If tomorrow brings one more day
Still no futures are on display
Until that day's end has found a way
To let me be, allowed to stay

But when my days have come to not
And in a sigh my last breath sought
When heaven's vote to cast its lot
To enter paradise or in hell to rot

A Summer Day

Oppressive heat of humid days
Restricts the tasks of labor
Ceaseless efforts to carry on
Are chores of much disfavor

Roiling clouds form and gather
Dark in swirls of stirring
Apprehensive of what's coming
Yet the cool moist air's alluring

A single drop, then more to come
The dusty paths soon laden
The storm of falling hissing rain
As the light of day is fading

Lighting flashes and thunder rolls
The wind breathes out its breath
Then too soon the storm has passed
And dripping leaves are left

Then the sun breaks forth anew
And awards with midday heat
Once again, the air's oppressive
And now there's mud beneath our feet

Spring Storms

The deep rumbling thunder rolls across the land, echoing from open window to open window. Rain pattering on the metal roof in rhythmic cycles interrupted only by the high-pitched call of an early morning bird.

From the upstairs window I can barely define the silhouette forms of the dark greens of spring framed by the blackened trunks of the rain-soaked trees.

A hint of gray light is beginning to illuminate the eastern horizon, and the celebration of morning is joined in with new calls from differing species of birds. Frogs in rain puddles advertise their desires.

An occasional puff of cool moist air wafts through the opened window, a welcome refreshment to the staleness of the night's closed shades.

The immediate surroundings are pleasant, quieted now after the violence of the invading cold front had surrendered its powers.

A remnant cloud in a hopeless cycle, attempting to develop into a new storm. It rises and falls in intensity as the failing winds go still.

Yes, the atmosphere is cozy and inviting, contrasting the warm and dry, against the wet and cool, just beyond the confining walls. Everything in life is right for the moment.

SELFISH CARING

I've stayed and lived, not for me, for conclusion is our fate
But so as not to shake your life I hesitate and wait
Should I premature my demise, and ignore your selfish plea
Can you make a sacrifice to set my suffering free

I strongly suspect your answers never in my interest
For only that which pads your life is what you will invest
As you grieve and lament my passing to tears that fill a sea
Consider that you put you first and not once considered me

Yet to your comfort I understand why you held me fast
Of those who've been of family tree I am your remaining last
So please find solace in knowing that I'm now free of my pain
Invest your hopes and prayers and dreams that we'll be family
once again

I Will Not Cry

Choking the words so not to betray the emotions of the moment
Yet betrayal broke through in the prolonged pause of silence
Faking a cough to hide the contorted heave of a sob
Forced composure allowed emotions to be reigned back and the crisis has passed
Diverting attentions to the trivial, escaping from the turmoil that lay just beyond the surface
The subject immediately resurrected, and the swell of pain rose to a greater level
Let it go, it cannot matter anymore, words burn deep, and attitudes are not forgotten
Allow that which was to die the quiet death of peace, leaving the struggle for survival at rest

Saying Goodbye

This day will last in memory until there are no more to come
The sun did shine, the breeze did stir, and all else as days are done
Unaware and void of concerns no people to come and go
But what should be expected of them for no one else could know

I walk the distance across the span from chiseled stone to stone
I stand beside the yawning earth, standing there alone
No one was invited for no one cared to grieve
I stand in silent reverence, not wanting that I should leave

My worries are your comfort, that you'll be safe and warm
The cold of night, the darkened tomb, a sentence to be borne
I pleaded you need not go, I begged to go with you
And now I waste useless days wishing I too were through

Tomorrow Is Now

"Celebrate," they say. For today is now. Tomorrow is but an unfulfilled promise of new opportunities. How does one make such long-term plans in the way of better tomorrows when confined to a body old and tired and frail with disease? Today is now and there in stands alone any prospects of the future. At least I still have this moment.

DIAMONDS OF PROMISE

Emerging from the cocoon of security, reaching for that illusive assurance that being has purpose, from nothing to everything.

Embedded deep within the soul is a praise clamoring to escape the lips of those who believe, but only for those who can see beyond the blinds of reality. Assurances of greater understanding fade like the light of stars as the brilliance of the dawning sun washes over the land and sky. That which brings clarity revealing truth dims and fades away as the points of star light vanish, believed to have been diamonds of promise.

GUILTY RAGE

A rage intent on casting shame in remembrances where regrets culminate into rivers of despair designed to entrap victims into a state of hopelessness. All is quiet now, my intentions lying in the ruins of broken determinations. Too late to utter words of remorse to those who wait in silent pain from what lay unfinished in life. What stands ready just beyond this moment, a moment that never finds its end?

MISSED OPPORTUNITIES

In quiet solitude the image of hope, a projection of the future decorated with scarce past triumphs stands starkly in the misty shadows of veiled failures. The representation looms, towering ominously over the moment with threatening clarity of unacknowledged opportunities. Oh, that I could have known what was truth in value, so I would have clutched your being to my heart in sacred reverence, never to let go.

CLOSING DOWN LIFE

Lament the loss of failed opportunities with profound regret
Yet cast away the dreams of planned successes, attempting to forget
Gather the fragments of broken promises and leave nothing up for chance
Resign ambitions to the fate of facts and quell the charged advance
Reticent in declaring fate for need of proved distinctions
Cluttered paths of unmarked signs defining unknown functions
Alone in private hopes and fears till all the thoughts are gone
At last, the purpose of life's walk, crests like distant dawn

THE SEARCH

I was set upon a journey to find those hidden treasures. Secrets restrain the heart and mind from the contentment of a fuller knowledge. That we are is easy to confirm. That we were, retraces what was until it fades into a mystery shrouded in the dark memories of nothingness. That we will be again is challenged by the silence of those who never return. Yet we continue to forge forward with hope inspired faith believing there is purpose, always intent to all things. Each day is consumed in looking but never seeing, listening but never hearing, reaching but never finding. The allusive door leading to the ultimate knowledge, an enlightenment that when found will open the gates of a reality never before imagined. But still I wait and wait, listening for the sounds of reason should they someday rise above the den of endless and distracting pursuits, white noise emitted from all of those who have given up on ever finding that illusive door.

THE TESTAMENT

My contribution is of great value in that I have a testimony only I can give. This testament is defining what it was like to be me living under my own unique circumstances. That is the testimonial offering we each have to give. No one can give any more of an offering to truth than an accurate recital as to whom and what he or she has been in life. Why judge one another? Our stories are not better one over another, just different.

Winter's Hell

Seasons cycle to opposing slants
A measure of God's decree
Weary of the vapid chance
Yet misery is still to be

Winds of unmatched savagery
Threatens dictums of frigid fate
Unveils impending adversity
Succors no planned escape

Fierceness that's void of amity
Assails the abandoned soul
Gives birth to all anxiety
Charging life to pay its toll

The scene imparts in full view
Much more than just a gale
The vicious winds that do ensue
Bears a taste of winter's hell

Touch that subject of denial
Trace its hidden form
Know perimeters in testing trials
Strive to not conform

A climb to reach the mountain top
The perspective of a king
Reveals a newfound truth of thought
That changes everything

THE TREASURE CHEST

Memorials of a life gone by tell of joys and triumphs, failures of a sorted nature, and unrequited love that had held the promise of eternity but now lay in a dust covered chest of broken and abandoned dreams.

Treasures of an age gone by measured in the value of experiences. A faded crumbling carnation flower pressed between the pages of a family Bible, held in time as a memorial of that loved one who could not receive the sentiment intended.

A collection of tributes and trinkets dedicated to a time of want that could not be attended to or satisfied and was left in a state of self-denial.

END OF THE LINE

The edges of my world close in around me, my awareness diminishes as the days of life drift into sunset. What was once an open range of limitless boundaries are now confined like the glowing ring of fire light that extends only into the immediate concerns. Many of those I've known have gone to a mysterious destiny and now I wait my turn with tired thoughts, fearful of the unknown. Is there more life beyond this or is it over? Was the experience just for this moment or is a greater purpose waiting to be exposed and expounded upon revealing an ultimate truth?

Not one of those who have gone has returned to let us know and as each moment of unsuccessful searching passes by, hope fades. "Next," I hear the doorman call. Now is my time to leave those loved ones behind as I have been left behind, clinging to an unknown, or not.

ALL THE SAME

You pass me on the street filled with strangers who might glance at my face but will not see me. I don't blame you, I can't blame, for I too see but don't see, and hear but don't hear. Yet sometimes when recognition happens, I smile in an attempt to get a smile in return and when it works, I celebrate.

When you don't smile in return, I feel bad. I wonder if it is because of me, how I appear to you, or is it that you are having a bad day, week, or life.

Sometimes you look away before I can flash a smile in your direction and sometimes, I look away because you look angry or are too pretty for me to risk the rejection of no returned smile. Sometimes I wish I could ask you what is so troubling in life that makes you look so profoundly sad. I would cry with you and share your heartache. I would tell you how valuable you are, not only in that you are you but also on a celestial level where some entity hidden in the heavens also holds you as precious.

Sometimes I don't care. Those are the times I am having a bad day, week, or life.

CLEAR TO SEE

Nonconform to the pattern of repetition. Be that stand-alone figure of unity, reflecting the body image of your mirrored configuration. Refuse to refuse and resist resisting, projecting self as the unique individual of unified harmony. Let no one mistake your identity as part of the unwavering symphony of sameness. For ours is unique in we wear different colors. Our team stands singularly apart from the redundancy of the rest. Together we are one, not as parts or of purpose, but single in our alikeness. When we pray for victory over our adversaries knowing they too are praying for victory over us, does it not confuse God?

STILL HERE

Celebrate as we did, the essence of liberty too soon has worn thin and dulled the brightness of promising futures. The realities of responsibilities have replaced much of the joys of life with the burdens of survival.

As children we had the best of all worlds, if held close by loving parents. It was a time we could not yet appreciate for lack of comparison.

Oh, that we could return to those days of carefree wonder and once again experience the newness of life that came with each waking day. How much more could we truly appreciate the values our worlds hold? If only we had the contrast to what is now to what could have been.

GROWING IN BIBLE WISDOM

I found a verse of mystique intrigue
Defined in words unknown
Efforts to render brought fatigue
Still meanings were not shown

The hour of one, and then of two
Time builds into a day
A week, a month, and years time grew
Till the verse was put away

Atop the shelf it sat a decade
Tempting in passing time
Mocking me with its charade
To know and make it mine

One quiet eve it enchanted so
I took it from its rest
Determined that I not let go
Vowed to give my best

That once hidden and estranged
Revealed to full engaged
Were not the words that met with change
But wisdom as I've aged

HOME

May death take us to a place where hope becomes truth
Freedom and joy not yet realized
Carry us to paradise where all things are made right
Banish from life the dreaded times that consumed us with so much uncertainty
Take us to the river that flows from beside the throne of God
Seat us in joyous crowds to never be alone
Bring us each to the place we all once knew as home

THE VICTIM

Expressions made in angry words of what's denied to feel.
Must not admit to thoughts of hate for what should not be real.
To cry, to weep, or tell of fear, defines them as so weak.
They won't be touched but should it be of such they dare not speak.

They have no rights to push away those in command.
With plaintiff voice they may object, yet yield, to the demand.
The doors then close so not to know or recognize regret.
When it is through and freedom comes, again they must forget.

Worn Paths

I thought to wage a journey
To destinies unknown
A place in time and geography
Where no one else has gone

Only to find in retrospect
The paths so worn and deep
I sat and grieved for my loss
Unbridled floods I weep

Still that ember deep in me
Will not flame out and die
Commands I not concede defeat
And wills again I try

So here I am, present to you
Those articles of unknown
Again, I try lest my will should die
In search of going home

Here in Hell

I think you should know
If ever questioned why
Today is not just a day
But the day on which I'll die

And should you have the questions
Of how this I should know
Is not that you should understand
But simply let it go

Yet on the morrow morning
If here you should still be
That now the chains are shattered
And of me you are set free

But should you too be broken
Of such you cannot tell
Just give your thoughts the token
And leave the traps of hell

Unanswered Questions

There's something dark in those woods,
the stand of trees beyond the edge.
It's not the person, the young man there,
but in the force that breaks the pledge.
Though never spoken, or given voice,
the promised trust was bound in faith
That you'd ever be here in this life,
an assumption you knew your place.
Yes, something evil lurks within
that forest just beyond the rim.
It imprisons the heart of one so young,
giving back the gift of life.
If those behind could have known,
they would have begged you not to go.

MISSING YOU

Stepping into wakefulness
To know you are no more
In shock again as first to learn
Revisited grief of loss
Anguished bitter pain
Shattered hopes and plans
Desperate to find saving grace
To soothe embittered souls
Why did you leave, so much beloved
No words to say 'goodbye'
A void of endless barren waste
Of where you were in life

COMMUNICATION

You, guised with feigned assertions
In garbs of forged concern
Did pronounce your sworn devotion
While in secret your ire did burn

Though I in pledge rewarded you
Allegiant to your claim
In secret I did scorn you
For never knowing shame

HEAVEN'S SHAME

I should think not to its shame
Heaven adds another name
To that infinite list of assigning fate

Thoughts we think to stand in line
Defying death in biding time
Hiding in ignorance of that date

In hopes, we hope that we're not doomed
Depending only on what's assumed
Praying our warnings aren't too late

DISCOVERING GOD

I wish that God would speak aloud
And tell us of His being
Not in words of sin and death,
But of hope and truth revealing.

Untold Secrets

It was a gift of measured worth
To those who never knew
A curse of imposed happenstance
From which the guidelines grew

Cautious vigilance, guarded space
Borders that confine
Prison walls forced to protect
Built by fears' design

They could not know, I could not tell
Define the reasons why
Restrictions laid right or wrong
They saw as freedoms denied

And now regret is mine to bear
In failures to inform
Of shame was why I could not share
Of dangers I knew to warn

WHO AM I

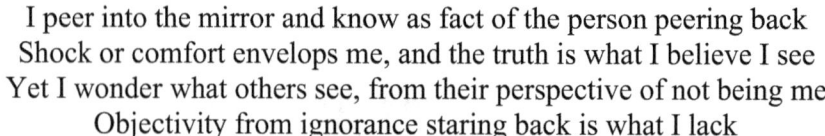

I peer into the mirror and know as fact of the person peering back
Shock or comfort envelops me, and the truth is what I believe I see
Yet I wonder what others see, from their perspective of not being me
    Objectivity from ignorance staring back is what I lack

    The eyes returning gaze to me, know the deeds of secrecy
    Of whom and what I could have been, the depths to which I can
        descend
No single one those could defend, family members or trusted friend
Can ever know the self that's me, the scenes I've seen and fantasies

    The fact there are two of me, the one I know and think to see
    Is not the one others understand, in truly knowing who I am
The deeds I've done, the poised sham, they cannot know me as that
        man
But then they see what I can't see and know the person that's part of
        me

    Should I come to know the me, what others see I can't see
    And forget the deeds I've done to offer a better one
Leave those truths of where I've gone, and those things of what I've
        done
    That the person I now see is just the one I'm known to be

    So what I see and know of me is not devoid of sympathy
    Now willing to extend a hand, based on what I understand
Reasons for the acts so vain that bear the depths of so much shame
To temper judgment of what I've been is to forgive myself and start
        again

The truth of who and what is me, to combine the two so I might see
Realize the one who knows the shame is also the one known by name
Was both right and wrong to cast blame, upon we who are each the same
To know my anger or see me as mild is to forgive the man and know the child.

THE REAPER'S TALENT

Should I rob the Reaper of his talent and his dues
Act upon my judgment of where and when I choose
It's not that I am selfish and think my knowledge prime
But slowness of the Reaper's work is more than I have time

With bated breath I hesitate to see what's coming next
Will some of what is wrong in life present a lasting fix
If I in agitation expedite my pending fate
Will it prove to have been better that I patiently await

The morrow as a mystery will not give up its plan
The only way to know what's next is to hope to understand
So here I sit conflicted as to which path be my fate
To know whether to stop or go for either I must wait

IF I HAD ONLY KNOWN

The sound of rain outside my window, a blended hiss of a million falling drops, fills the quiet of the early evening. We sit in front of the pulsating monitor displaying the contents of a running computer. Searching for the treasures of life to be expressed in eloquent words, the utterances fall short of delivering the value of what is there. Only in hindsight is the measure of worth realized, too late to make known the full extent of appreciation to those who can no longer know.

I find myself longing to be in that time and place where a greater degree of contentment could have and would now be cherished moment by moment. I didn't know what I had when it was within my reach, and now those persons may be gone forever. My tortured regrets plague my anguished soul with a chastising reprimand, and curses escape my lips, condemning me of my foolishness.

I wish God would step in and rescue this miserable world. I don't know how to stop hating my existence in this love barren wilderness. If I could, I would fix everything for everyone and then celebrate the victory in exposing all the distortions and blatant lies.

DARE TO QUESTION

We were taught to think no thoughts, deeper than the day.
Ignorance is where we started and where we are to stay.
Never ask the source of life beyond the act of love,
Why skies are blue or clouds are gray or what might lie above.
Nor look beneath the budding wings of a merging butterfly,
Don't challenge God to know His art and *never* ask Him why.

What could it hurt to turn a stone, to view the mysteries hidden,
Why should questions anger God to inquire of that's forbidden?
A hoard of bugs and crawling worms, escaping from the light,
Or search the heavens, to know the stars that adorn the skies of night,
So, when allowed an armor's chink to open the mind,
Pull back the veil for just a peek to learn what lies behind.

Should man ask to know of more, dare to be so bold,
Or does God hold His mystique secrets, keeping man controlled?
Beyond the words of supposition, knowledge yet concealed,
Search through that of each generation, holds as truth revealed,
Offering nothing of tangible proof to support their determinations,
Declaring theirs as final truth, all else as abominations.

Should dare ask, look beyond those oracles of sacred precision,
For lies and ignorance are the same that fosters trust's division.
Is not man imbued with quests to leave no stone unturned,
Construct monuments of gained knowledge, built on all that's learned?
From a new perspective, see a truth that evil has long disguised
It's not of God to hide the truth but through Christ to be realized.

Rewards

If tomorrow doesn't bring relief
And today still stays equal,
'Tis not promised in the way of better
In vestige note of sequel.

By early morn, one's sure to know
If not of midday too,
If progress moves up or down
Or if the time is through.

Only as I feel my way
From doubt to confidence,
Can the truth, on full display
Declare a recompense.

LEARNING GRACE

Said God of His creation plan,
To crown His art with defective man,
So that in the end, God is to blame,
For all the woes of bearing shame.

Destined is His artistry to fail,
A knowledge of, but to no avail.
The task at hand is all the cause,
Rethought designs warrant no pause.

Beauty is His deep intent,
Where all His best can be spent,
To form a subject of admired perfection,
Where all He is in man's reflection.

Aware that life would come to naught,
Appears to have no care or thought,
For failure seemed His intended aim
Presenting ruin and awarding shame.

Yet, why would God design an error
Crafting man to end in terror?
Was not to smear His imaged face,
But to reveal His loving grace.

WAITING ROOM

I do not worship wealth or fame
Or practice any pompous games
For pretentious demeanor on display,
Will come to naught some fateful day.

Into the ground or ash or crypt
Or ocean depths allowed to slip,
It matters not to those who sleep
For all they were not theirs to keep.

But while I live and know this place,
I hold to hope to learn of grace,
And know that death is not the doom,
But simply heaven's waiting room.

LESSONS IN HOPE

A withered corn kernel, I hold in my grip,
A tribute to death, an ugly misfit,
Distorted and gnarled, contorted in twists,
To plant the poor thing is taking a risk.

I waste precious energy, wouldn't you know,
That the hideous dead thing is not going to grow,
But not one to give up, daily I peek,
And low and behold it sprouts in a week.

Encouraged and hopeful I tend to its needs,
Cultivating the soil and clearing the weeds,
Taller and taller it surpasses my height,
The stocks of deep green grow taller at night.

Then the day comes to harvest the ears,
A small celebration of triumphs and cheers,
I clean way the husks and pick the silk hair,
And invite a dear friend with which I will share.

What once lay in my hand so dead and so frail,
Gave us such pleasure to go with our meal.
The lesson I learned is to keep a good thought,
And to think what can be rather than not.

SELLING A SOUL

The ambient consensus
That truth is no concern.
Are favored for consignment
Ill-gotten and not earned.

The soul is placed upon the block
Of fraudulence and of deep shame.
To cover all the hidden lies
Attributed to your name.

The power that has changed the wills
Once appeared as principled and fair,
Were threats to open long-kept secrets,
To voters make aware.

That truth and noble character
Was not your path to fame,
But deals of crass corruption
Are listed by your name.

What is in a Color?

I dislike the color purple when it decorates the skin,
It speaks of pain and injury where a violent act has been.
The color red is bloody or in traffic makes me stop,
Yet it signifies harvest time of a sweet strawberry crop.
I scorn the color yellow as defining race or courage
Or as signals of the coming cold as Aspens lose their foliage.
A sky of blue can be too much in the blazing summer sun,
Relief coming only when the long hot day is done.
And the color green is known of envy and of spite,
Leading to a confrontation, resulting in a fight.
But most of all the pigment colors when combined of every hue,
Red, orange, yellow, pink, and all the colors too,
Contained within this resulting color where no color does it lack.
I fear the color blue: I fear the color black.
Yet when these colors are projected as a beam of light
The combination of them all renders the color white
An empty image of nothing that lacks contrasting blend
No projections of a picture no beginnings and no end
But what I fail to recognize, in this mixture of the whole,
Is what makes this world's beauty appealing to the soul.
So why should I hate a color whether white or black or blue?
For everything has its meaning and has its unique hue.
So when it comes to valuing whether uniform or skin,
The truth of what to love or fear is what there is within.

FILLING A VOID

The winds of winter circle,
Outside the darkened room.
In swirls of cold currents,
Murmuring predictions of my doom.

The shutters creak with movement,
As I cower in my bed.
Covers pulled up tightly,
Concealing all but just my head.

I pull the sheet up tighter,
Shielding all but peeking eyes.
Tuck my feet beneath the borders,
Of the blanket sides.

I whisper words of comfort,
To no one else but me.
Squinting hard in the darkness,
To see what I can see.

Shadows of a spirit,
Fly down from atop the door.
Spreading like a liquid,
Across the bedroom floor.

A stench of rotting flesh,
Assaults my sense of smell,
Crawls up beside my body,
As far as I can tell.

A rumbling in the hallway,
A light beneath the door.
The turning of the knob,
I plead out my implore.

It's Mother, she's inquiring
Why do I cry out in the night
I mutter "Just leave the light on,
And I will be alright."

FADING VISIONS

Sunbeams defused in scattered stains.
The grime of once clear windowpanes,
Distorts the scenes beyond the glass.
Reminds the heart of blurring past.

Reminiscent of times and places,
Fading memories of all those faces,
Instills a panic that I might lose,
Those precious images of you I choose.

As the verities in life obscure,
Facts of memories become unsure.
And like the smudged window view,
So is the countenance that once was you.

Sign Post

I came upon a sign one day,
Inviting me to walk its way.
Contemplating what to do,
Uncertain of to go or stay,
Was told to choose, not delay.
The choice was one and not two,
No surprise, I always knew.

Stepping first onto that path,
No shadows did my person cast.
Blithe in hopes a destined free,
Of impending latent wrath,
A second step beyond the last,
Opens to an endless sea,
Peopled with no one but me.

ALOOF

Bars imprison, walls confine,
All are bordered in its kind,
Pretense, a world of no restrain,
Endless cycles of freedom feigned.

Promises swore as fate and fact,
Boundaries ruled and kept exact,
No limits to stymie, all open and free,
Imagined fantasies for theirs and for me.

Visions of light shrouded in dark,
Contrasted as two, both rigid and stark,
Only to fade into blends of the same,
No longer defined, nor labeled by name.

Search of the heavens, for truth absolute,
Appointments of labor imposed constitute,
Deficient of answers, of tangible proof,
The Sacred and Holy, remaining aloof.

ENIGMA

I can feel the color red as it lies beyond my reach
I smell the sounds of touching that life can never teach
I taste the winds that stir the leaves into eddies in the yard
I see the thoughts of wisdom, as the face of time is scarred
I hear the sweet of nectar that pours out from the sun
I sense the passing stillness, as time is here but gone
I listen to the clouds as they drift across the sky
I touch the edge of nothing though I never question why
But most of all I'm eager to taste the letter three
And know the sounds of colors that touching cannot see
Simple complex lost on sight, waiting for the dawn of night
Sit standing on the minute vast, arriving early at a time that's past
Confused clarity of certain doubt, to know what nothing is about
Hold tight the freedom of restrain, and give to suffering the joy of pain

DANCING STARS

An evening's walk, dark country road
Steps of cautious measure
To top of hill my pathway strolled
Revealed a summer's treasure

A scene of heaven that's fell to earth
Filled the valley floor
A twinkling of the stars in birth
Ten thousand lights and more

Mesmerized I stood in awe
This marriage of earth and skies
So captivated in what I saw
The dancing of fireflies

QUICK TO JUDGE

One eve attending a social meet
A mix match of attendees
I strolled casually along the street
When I encountered a small assemblage

Watching a storm of distant skies
The audience of three
Threats of violence as sunlight dies
Ends the day of gentle breeze

Standing behind the watching crowd
I too felt deep distress
Of my concern I voiced aloud
To which not one of them addressed

'How rude' I thought, 'unfriendly too'
My feelings had been hurt
And soon my anger did ensue
In search of words to blurt

Ignore me in my friendly reach
To bond as humankind
I'll retort in bitter speech
I'll give them a piece of mind

Then one of them took note of me
And asked of me by choice
Spoke with hands that I could see
In a monotone
of voice

Ask me what of my concern
Was the storm of need to fear
Was only then I came to learn
Not one of them could hear

MOM

A formless ghost hovers near, words cannot define.
Intellectually you're not here, except in memories of your time.
The corner chair, the scuffed imprints of where your feet did rest,
Treasured trinkets and pictured walls so much of you expressed.

Suspended in silence, the motionless clock with no one to reset,
Hangs upon the wall of time as the beginnings of regret.
So much unsaid, so much undone, to tell of emptiness,
Nowhere to turn, or place of escape or comfort to address.

PHOBIA

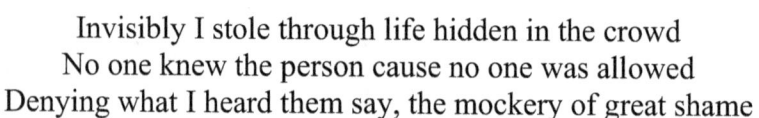

Invisibly I stole through life hidden in the crowd
No one knew the person cause no one was allowed
Denying what I heard them say, the mockery of great shame
I recoiled and faded to opaque blank as one that had no name

Ashamed to be embarrassed, contrite I could not change
Destined as a social freak, an outcast labeled *strange*
The center piece of ridicule a subject of cruel scorn
A mantle imposed upon my being assigned that it be worn

Beyond my view of barred escape of theirs they could not see
The reticent stance not mine by choice nor chose to not be free
Devoid of logic, of common sense their ignorance made them blind
Except they've walked the path I've walked *my* truth they'll never find

FADING LIFE

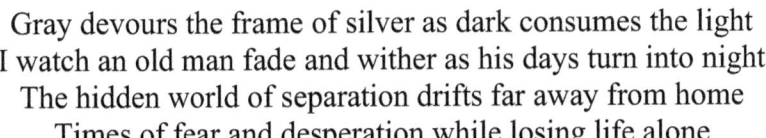

Gray devours the frame of silver as dark consumes the light
I watch an old man fade and wither as his days turn into night
The hidden world of separation drifts far away from home
Times of fear and desperation while losing life alone

His moments of grand celebration have peaked and fell to earth
Loves of promised determination held as precious worth
Crumbling pieces of broken plans now dust upon the wind
Bewildered to know and understand why time refused to mend

Remnants of that time now hang in frayed disguise
The gray of truth clouds the image, obscures the blue of skies
The old man fights the war of grief his beloved dog dims and fades
Now lays at rest beneath the ground, under shadows of tree shade

Dedicated to Jim

BECOMING A MAN

At 17 he was a child, adult things were forbidden
He could not vote, he could not drink, most vices remained hidden
Then 18 happened in a single day, one day from child to man
Yet he'd not changed in 24 hours, he's still who he has been

The shift was not in what he wanted but demands that were decreed
Each passing day from time forward fulfilling commands of need
Drafted into a world not his, he was ordered to kill or die
Those promises of a glory post turned out to be a lie

He learned to fade into the scene and blend within the frame
Where a number rank and status replaced that was his name
And when the time to return from war a journey coming home
He discovered the child he was, was abandoned and all alone

The care they promised to help him mend and gain some that was lost
Delivered as a commodity failed to address his cost
The price he paid in the fields of hell where life was valueless
His coming home has been a need to hide in stark distrust

And now that time is but history and settled in its place
The war still rages within him, yet hidden in his face
The wounds still unhealed and sensitive to thought
Had choice been his to age or stay, to age he would have not

PUBLIC OPINION

The subject of derision stands docile at the gate
A place where all the citizens come to congregate
An unofficial body of those who magistrate
Always at the ready with threats to castigate

Guilt or not of no concern, accusation equals fault
They hold the key to his freedom or to seal him in a vault
The victim holds no powers to fend off their assault
His pleas for mercy and claims of innocence gain him no result

---

SAYING GOODBYE

How does one say 'goodbye' to the constant of a lifetime, watch in anguished silence as the embodiment of years of shared experiences is transported out the door disappearing like a fleeting thought?

How can the echoes of all the past become unheard, fade away into a storybook of tales and pretended imaginations that in truth do matter?

How does one carry on in the plans of tomorrow when tomorrow is missing so much of the plan?

This is the substance of life, denied prospects of future accomplishments and cancellations of purpose in search of meaningful distractions to fill the voids of loss.

THE PINNACLE OF KNOWLEDGE

Suddenly, a field of orange and green rises to my plane of vision and I behold the scene with baited curiosity.

"Why orange and green?" The question disturbs my security of ignorance. I am satisfied to remain placated in this space I have carved out in the cleft of incognizance which keeps me so sedately satisfied and far removed from that world of 'what and why.' I have purposefully remained segregated, isolated from the vacillatory state of troubling challenges for questions that tend to confound my world of unquestionable acceptance. I am happy. I don't want waves. The tossing to and fro tends to upset my gentle nature and remaining in ignorance is my most coveted escape. "Why indeed? DON'T MAKE ME THINK!"

Yet in time my resistance was to no avail and a new horizon had been introduced. A question began to form, and I soon found myself mystified with the curiosity of what light illuminated the distant peaks of the unknown.

A new me was beginning to surface and I was quite frankly scared. I ducked back into my world of safe naivete, a world that didn't challenge the definitive proclamation of those who claimed to have forehand knowledge where the first rule was not to challenge.

In surrender, I began to reject the widely accepted consensus and started using my God given abilities to think. I had begun a long journey of attempting to make their accepted pieces of the puzzle fit my sense of what seemed to be the most logical and reasonable.

And so…
I scan the pieces scattered about
Comparing space to likened shape
And when a find appears to fill the gap
I attempt to place it in that space
The jagged edges fail to match

And even though the piece will not conform
I turn and push and turn again
Notwithstanding how I try
The fit is awkward and incomplete
I give up and admit my defeat

Again, I scan for space and part
Find a portion to place as apt
As before I turn and push
Ignoring sides that fail to match
Blame the misfit upon itself
Refuse to acknowledge the fault as mine
Nor admit to the waste of time
Forgive the piece of stubbornness
Resume the task of the search
Scan to match for space to place
At last resigned to their defeat

    It has taken me many years to work my way out of the 'thought prison' I had been entombed in since the beginning. Freedom is relative and I was becoming free of myself. But without fail there were always the revisiting scenes of the tragedies and each return devastatingly brutal that escape was often in serious jeopardy. But escape I did and in time the lessons of why I kept going back began to solidify into a greater understanding of myself.

    I needed to believe in God. God represents 'hope' and hope is as fundamental to human existence as is breathing. A life devoid of hope is destined to resign in defeat and defeat is the enemy of all projections toward a future. At every given moment in life the only perspective of positive is to embrace the next moment and the next and the next...

    From my vantage point, of the orange and green valley floor, my line of sight began to climb to greater heights reaching towards the unknown. Soon I found myself needing to know what was beyond the known. I began making my ascent into the heavens of the secrets of truth, a truth based on facts of cause and effect rather than of fear driven faith that resides in a place of desperate emotionalism.

Much of my journey has been tracing over the pathways of so many before me. As I climbed, I grew to hold some of these great minds of wonder in high esteem. Minds that dare to challenge the status quo of beliefs even in the face of deadly retributions.

I am sorely tempted to denigrate the images of those purveyors of blind faith, yet to do so would constitute an effort to remove a very essential portion to the equation of truth. 'Challenge' is the fundamental of exploration and without the definitive proclamation of those who claim to know, the desire to expose a greater truth might well have never risen to the occasion. Making the absolute declaration should never garner a response of blind acceptance.

So, I have challenged the subject of Godliness with the reason and logic of all the 'what and why' to know, yes even to know the mind of God.

As the mountain of knowledge is scaled there begins to surface the realization that nothing in the universe has been left up to 'chance.' Atomic particles did not wander on to the scene and in some mysterious way decide to circle the nuclei thus forming the 'atom.' And even in the event this was the case, then what unapplied force prompted the first atom to propagate and diversify into what now exists? 'Dictates' suggest purpose, purpose brings results, and results form foundations upon which to further the dictates of purpose.

The theory of 'evolution' is not a valid argument of pinpointing our origin. The faith needed to believe time arranged all conceivable scenarios is subject to the afore-mentioned challenge. It is possible I could take a coin from my pocket and in a 'heads or tails' challenge toss the coin a googolplex number of times, and each time the resultant win would be 'heads.' Yet, in reality, the likelihood of that being the case is infinitely remote. That is unless the coin has been programmed to always be on the winning side. If that's the case, then who did the programming?

As I am ascending to the mountaintop of knowledge, what will I discover at the pinnacle of truth? Dare I hope a discovery reveals the ultimate Scientist reclining in a Kingly repose, whom addresses me with a single question, "I've been waiting for you. What took you so long?"

I Cannot Let it Go

Pull back the mask, know I am not what I pretend to be.

The stern pride of a rigid jaw, indifference expressed with the cold blank stare of eyes that have no soul. I stand in strong opposition, condemning the lies of empathy. I cannot let it out. I cannot let it go. Too completely I have clutched the fragile truth hidden within this heart of stone, and still, I cannot let it go.

I won't cry. I won't let them see me hurt. I won't give them the victory of knowing they have driven a fatal arrow through the heart of feigned stone, wounding me unto death. Yet, I cannot let it go.

Let them fall from their grace of ignorance and let them believe in the lies.

Yet, I cannot reach the depth of soul that grieves for the loss of self. I cannot find me. I cannot let it go.

CHILD IN NEED

I don't know how to speak of these deep secrets of my heart
Define the battered spirit's state while acting out my part
I ask you not scold me for my need to run away
Or shower me with shame and guilt to try and make me stay

Before you judge me, walk my path to know and understand
The child who was disposable, who never grew to man
Although I did my duties as society decreed
I never could reveal the child and how much he was in need

REWARDS OF LIFE

I am ill and tired and weak with a temperature too high
My body has an enemy that wants me to fade and die
I told the people in my life I was sick and did not feel well
Some looked at me, shrugged at my plea, and told me 'enjoy hell'

The Folly of Youth

At birth the page is clean, free of marks though bordered with constraints that will soon be defined as open or closed doors of opportunity. The infant's cries of discomfort grow into incoherent babbling, then to simple words of protest, and in time evolve into ultimatums of demand. Of course there are joyous moments too.

Later in life, with a head full of life's unfolding events and exacting responsibilities, the budding adult wishes to dull to blank where nothing stirs the emotions of sentiment and where nothing cares about anything, then the slow and mysterious transformation changes everything.

It seems every generation, while still full of youthful ambitions, believe that mocking the old of years is clever, that being brash and disrespectful gains them an advantage. Not realizing that calling out shouts of disdain from their fortification of ignorance is the embodiment of obtuseness. While recognizing the young and foolish are dearth of wisdom, and they not realizing I too walked their path not long ago. I choose to discount their opinions. Knowledge gained in time is the enemy of benightedness.

THE EIGHTH DEADLY SIN

Lies should be held in deep disdain and for those who lie or misrepresent the truth of truths their acts should not go unpunished. A lie is a deliberate attempt to barter ignorance and knowledgeable truth. Marketing deceptions are solely for the gain of those who practice such. If there was true justice in this world there would be an accounting of the act of lying punishable up to a sentence of imprisonment, perhaps death, according to damages the lies have done. Lying should be counted as the *eighth* deadly sin.

BURIED TREASURES

I should think we all can agree there are still many hidden truths of our universe that are treasures yet to be discovered. If there is a treasure buried in my back yard it means someone buried it there.

CANCER

I could not have guessed who would be calling, beckoning at my gate
Me, toiling with the plans of life, goals and duties that would not wait
The stranger addressed me with gestured moves, he did not ask admission
Passing through the entry way he advanced without permission
Drifting towards my place of standing he floated through the air
Towering over my full stature, menacingly he stared
From his dark hooded shroud his voice was harsh and deep
He announced there was a date for me demanding that I keep

DENIAL

Tell yourself the lies you most want to hear
Lies prompted by indifference to be wholly unaware
Though you know beyond the surface the facts of what is real
You refuse to look beneath the cover of what you do conceal

To every story there comes a page that does not support denials
And opens a court of conscience that tests the truth in trials
Putting the long-concealed reality starkly in your face
Tearing down your feigned defense and causing you disgrace

THE BLISS OF STAGNATION

The amass of evil grime clouds thoughts of purity
As the model of time slips beneath the moment
I watch the people stagger to and fro bearing the aggregate of their history
Yet the stillness of that bygone narrative quivers in the wake of once being an imagination of reality never to know the time of its own favor
A storm of worry eats away at the edge of security as the reveal of truth threatens
I call out to the vestige of sanctity to impress a fragile hope only to experience more of the savageness of reality.
This moment fades into memories to be filed away with all the other retrospection that now offer no substance to change.
What was is not now and now is not what was and to the dolt the usefulness of knowledge fails to reveal the advantages of ignorance.
Holding to the assertion it does not help to know for knowing is being and being is filled with the fear of not being.
And the fool goes merrily along in a state of incognizant bliss

ESCAPING

Idly waiting, for a change of course
Sheltered from the threat
Shielded from the biting wind
Reject the pity of my fate
The only warmth comes from my breath
As the stranger bends near my face
Offering escape from this certain death
So, I traded pride for a handful of pills
My hope to quell despair
But when the change failed to be
I took another as a dare
Six pills later my world is spinning, and the cold has gone away
I could not recognize the self that's me or tell of night or day
Into a sleep of nearing death, I lie upon the floor
Against the doorway to this room asleep or maybe more
A sudden light breaks my world, disrupts the utter darkness
Again, to illuminate I am still alone
Questions tormenting my soul
What loathsome thing prowls in wait
Or joyous gift to treasure
Granted of enduring favor
All tomorrows, if granted more
Is but time's expired reflection
Days gone past that failed to last
Of daunting tasks or pleasures
Another pill I slip away from this pit of hell
Drifting into the great unknown
The dark horizon rises high obscuring the light of hope
At last, I fade into the past while trying to learn to cope

Escaping Self

Anticipation grows with every step as the journeys' goal looms far in the distance. Will there be all the attributes that dance in the visions of my hopes where every day is warm but not hot, cool but not cold, and moist but not drenched?

Are the trees and bushes laden with fruits and nuts, will the ground yield up the bounties of her making, and will the waters be sweet and refreshing?

And the people there, do they recognize me and call me by name, a place where I am no longer a stranger among strangers?

Paradise is projected in my mind's eye as the brightness of a thousand suns illuminating from horizon to horizon revealing the creatures, docile and without threat, roaming the fields, hills, plains and forests, interacting with man and nature in celebration of life and living.

The aromas of a garden of potential nectars promising to enhance the pleasure of taste and stimulate the senses, readily recognized as beneficial to the experience of feasting on unlimited offerings.

Another step and new visions scroll within my imaginations where exploration is an endless adventure into the unknown. Danger is a threat of the past and discovery is a continual turning of the pages of searching every mystery beneath layers of that which has yet to be learned.

What are now measured in steps of this journey are soon to be boundless in time where cycles will stretch beyond eternities.

But then I stop and pause to measure progress. What I see shakes my musings of confidence and hope, as the coveted goal appears to have advanced apart from me. I take one step, and my destination has taken two or more away from me. What is there about me that is so unlovely as to inspire goodness to flee my advances? Should I turn and walk the reverse? Will my destiny follow? How can I know?

Try, I must try, and so I spin around facing away from that which holds my desire and much to my horror I discover my past has been following close behind, about to overtake me.

I whirl about and with fear driven determination I begin to race towards that which shines promising in the greater distance. Time is breathing hot against the back of my neck and the pounding of my feet echo a rising chant of 'get away, get away' and my joys of hope transform into desperate fears of despair. That which was filled with great anticipation has marred into a pathway of escape.

In desperation my soul cries out to the great unknown. "Help me and free me, from these chains of shame. Release me from this guilt of ignorance for never having known. Remove me from this pit of hell, soar me above the confines of gravity, and give me freedom, true freedom that sheds the burden of being me."

Suddenly, my feet lose the force of friction, and my legs spin helplessly, expending pointless effort against a non-existent stratum. The sensation of floating dazzles my senses and I realize all powers to project myself have been taken away. I go limp and allow the forces of weightlessness to have their way with me. Turning my head, I see my past jumping to reach me only to fall back into confining memories that encompass an unsuccessful dying attempt to make me pay the price.

Again, I see my destination drawing closer as I am carried to that paradise of eternity.

A House of Words

Words, whether stated or in print, are but an instrument to convey information and ideas.
Words of themselves have never provided sustenance for hunger, not even for a child. They do not offer shelter from the cold rains of fall, nor do they offer protection from the snows of winter.
Words do not render safety from the fierceness of howling winds or cover for the threat of lighting.
Words do not provide shade from the blistering sun of late summer.
Words fail to plow the fields or plant the seeds or water the sprouts.
Words cannot fix the broken-hearted or terrified child.
Words are of no use when the fences need mending or repairs are needed for the buildings that provide shelter.
Words cannot move a stone or build a road or deliver a package.
Words are useless in accomplishing any task in the physical world.
Words are simply noises when spoken and marks upon a paper when written.
Words are for those who are thought to be foolish for believing in hopes and promises.
Words are for lovers and haters, those who condemn and those who forgive.
Words speak on a deeper level of who I am and are instrumental in building trust.
Words are not needed when we are alone, yet they can be the pathways to togetherness.
Yet words, if allowed to inspire, can accomplish all things.

ASSESSING VALUES

Our world is breaking down as the battle between human decency and greed inspired selfishness raise to new levels of social awareness, ultimately creating divisions between citizens, friends, and families. The issue is money, the instrument used to define the contents of men's hearts. It is a tool of power that exposes the true character of individuals.

Yet it is no wonder humans hold the importance of money as equal to or above all else in life. Many people are always standing at the ready to abandon the sacredness of life for the security of wealth. And why not? From childhood we are taught having lots of money should be the primary goal in life. We respond as we invest the greater portion of our existence in this futile and egregious pursuit. Societies proclaim it is having money that defines each our own sense of self-worth. To have none, labels one as a parasite on society. To have copious amounts means one can command others to be subservient and subject to those demands that pass money down through the chain of social status.

Yet in the end we all die. For those who believe in life after death there will be accountability as to how one controlled their riches. They either clutched in greed or shared their powers of money. Jesus defined human conduct consisting as one of two categories. Either one was unselfish and generous with their means, or they selfishly ignored the plight of those victims who were confined to the bottom of the social/financial pile. Sheep or goats, the decision is ours to make in accordance with the level of compassion we allow to control our conduct.

And whether one believes in the words in the Scriptures or not, there is the sense of being a decent human, allowing for the unfortunate that can happen to anyone at any time.

Allegedly to have originated from a mid-sixteenth-century statement by John Bradford, "There but for the grace of God, go I."

REAL MEN CRY

I watched the questioning and testimonies of those investigating the insurrection that occurred at the Capitol Building in Washington D.C., on January 6, 2021.

I watched and witnessed the deep heartfelt emotions of both the questioners and those police officers that had endured the brunt of the melee. Several of the officers expressed fierce anger at the indifferent attitudes of some of the Congressmen and Senators. Some of these testifying persons openly wept as they recounted their experiences.

Several of the questioning members of Congress wept too, as they addressed the bravery and selflessness of those gallant men who risked their lives protecting all the members of Congress, even those who so denigrated the officers' contributions of securing the safety for all. Those congressmen, who blatantly dismissed the gift these officers risked, stand in stark contrast of their obvious cowardice.

Watching these grown men openly weep touched a cord deep within myself and I too wept. If I had been in their company at that moment, I would have offered an assuring embrace recognizing their compassion and commitment to protecting the sacredness of a prevailing democracy.

I was taught crying was for children and women. A real man does not allow his feelings to interfere with business. A real man expresses his feelings as opinions and known facts and leaves the emotionalism to the ladies. A real man stands strong in the face of adversity and yields to nothing that betrays the child within.

Disciplining my inner child has always been a stumbling stone to my abilities to be a public speaker. Try as I may to corral that child, he would not accept the confinement and would invariably bubble to the surface and leave me embarrassed as I hopelessly attempted to stifle those tears. I would stand in front of a judging audience, whether of a single individual or a multitude of persons, and spend long silent moments struggling to gain my composure. The exhibition of lacking self-control furthered my embarrassment and prolonged my unsightly display of unbridled emotions. I have since avoided being the center of attention for this very reason. Even though I have lots to say I lack the discipline to say it in front of a live audience.

I have often been in the presence of men who readily allow their emotions to express themselves by shedding tears and at times was duly embarrassed for some of them. Other times I would be caught up in the moment and would join in, still attempting to hide what I could of my perceived display of unmasculine weakness.

My dad had struggled with alcoholism throughout his adult life and would often, when under the influence, express his otherwise denied pains and disappointments as a 'crying drunk.' I had seen this expression of inebriated sorrow many times and had grown impervious to his drunken blubbering. Then one time I witnessed my father openly expressing in total sobriety the pain he felt as I left to return to my residence in another state after vacationing at his home. Something I had never seen my dad do, not even at the funeral of his mother. My fortitude to remain complacent broke, and I wept with him, allowing the child within full reign of control. I can still tear up recalling that moment.

I don't know how many men share the same sentiment as I but obviously some don't.

This past spring I attended my granddaughters' high school graduation and was movingly impressed with the candidness of one of the male speakers. A man recounted the recent passing of his father, then suddenly took a long pause and announced to the audience, "I'm crying." I thought how absolutely refreshing it was to witness the open honesty of expressing the feelings of his inward child.

So, watching these men of high political positions, and those who work in careers of law enforcement, which is considered to be macho, giving vent to their emotions was refreshing and rewarding, instilling confidence in those who passionately defend the freedoms of all Americans.

To Be a Man

"You have a son." The words defined me to my parents and the world at large. Encompassing a litany of characteristics society recognized as being far more than a three-lettered word. Masculine, a fighter of a testosterone induced nature, attempting to construct a niche in the hierarchy of boyhood, and establishing self in a way that solidifies a pattern to last a lifetime.

Human male, body hair that's more than pubic or armpit, hair on legs, chest, back, and most notable facial. Nipples, but no breasts. Being a male almost guarantees an industrious libido that pushes and pulls and dictates social attitudes, pursuits, and actions. Though the objects of affection are not always in accordance with society's expectations.

Effort defines strength. Accomplishments define manhood. Someone forgot to tell me what a man is supposed to resemble. My response is to attempt to deflect the blame for not living up to conformity, but it is not I alone who appears to have lost the way.

A man has a propensity to kill rather than heal. A man curses those challenges in life that fail to comply with his will rather than finessing the object of intent into compliance. A man stands alone as a tower of undaunted strength, staunchly weathering the foes of safety and securities, assuring defenses unto the death.

A man is defined as that fortified tower of strength. I, as a man am but a child in denial. Bravery is following duty, allegiance is but uniformity, and honor is a response to the command of a heart that loves.

THE CYCLE OF SEASONS

The season of fall, though not mine alone
Chills of night air sweeps away the warmth of life
Confirming the days of coming dormancy
As the green of spring descends
Into the depths of faded functions
And time ticks by marching toward new cycles
But tomorrow's resurrection is a promise yet to be realized
And even as it materializes much too soon, summer's heat invades
with suffocation culminating into the dry tears of drought
For now, too is the season to weep in all that is being dismantled.
And still no bright horizons illuminate hopes of confidence

WOULD YOU STOP FOR ME

If I should reach out to you
And ask you hold me tight
Would you stop the thing you're doing
To help me feel alright

If I should speak of broken hearts
That plagues me with much grief
Would you stop the thing you're doing
To give my heart relief

If I should tell you of my intent
To resign this life of dread
Would you stop the thing you're doing
To give me love instead